CAMBRIDGE LIBRARY COLLECTION

Books of enduring scholarly value

History

The books reissued in this series include accounts of historical events and movements by eye-witnesses and contemporaries, as well as landmark studies that assembled significant source materials or developed new historiographical methods. The series includes work in social, political and military history on a wide range of periods and regions, giving modern scholars ready access to influential publications of the past.

Letters Written in France, to a Friend in London

Watkin Tench (1758–1833) was a British Marine officer who was held prisoner from 1794 to 1795 in Brittany, at the height of the French Revolution. During his imprisonment he wrote a series of letters to a friend in London (it is not clear whether this was genuine correspondence or a genre narrative), which was published in 1796. In them we learn of the adverse conditions he experienced on two convict hulks in Brest harbour, and his later period of parole in private lodgings in Quimper, which he recalls more favourably, as he was allowed to roam the countryside within a three-mile radius of the town. Tench's letters reveal his thoughts on the turbulence and uncertainty brought about by the revolution, and the resistance (largely inspired by religion) of the Bretons to it. This is a fascinating first-hand account of France at a time of rapid political change.

T0370940

Cambridge University Press has long been a pioneer in the reissuing of out-of-print titles from its own backlist, producing digital reprints of books that are still sought after by scholars and students but could not be reprinted economically using traditional technology. The Cambridge Library Collection extends this activity to a wider range of books which are still of importance to researchers and professionals, either for the source material they contain, or as landmarks in the history of their academic discipline.

Drawing from the world-renowned collections in the Cambridge University Library, and guided by the advice of experts in each subject area, Cambridge University Press is using state-of-the-art scanning machines in its own Printing House to capture the content of each book selected for inclusion. The files are processed to give a consistently clear, crisp image, and the books finished to the high quality standard for which the Press is recognised around the world. The latest print-on-demand technology ensures that the books will remain available indefinitely, and that orders for single or multiple copies can quickly be supplied.

The Cambridge Library Collection will bring back to life books of enduring scholarly value (including out-of-copyright works originally issued by other publishers) across a wide range of disciplines in the humanities and social sciences and in science and technology.

Letters Written in France, to a Friend in London

*Between the Month of November 1794,
and the Month of May 1795*

WATKIN TENCH

CAMBRIDGE
UNIVERSITY PRESS

CAMBRIDGE UNIVERSITY PRESS

Cambridge, New York, Melbourne, Madrid, Cape Town,
Singapore, São Paolo, Delhi, Tokyo, Mexico City

Published in the United States of America by Cambridge University Press, New York

www.cambridge.org
Information on this title: www.cambridge.org/9781108035361

© in this compilation Cambridge University Press 2011

This edition first published 1796
This digitally printed version 2011

ISBN 978-1-108-03536-1 Paperback

LETTERS

WRITTEN IN FRANCE,

TO A

FRIEND IN LONDON,

BETWEEN THE MONTH OF NOVEMBER 1794.

AND

THE MONTH OF MAY 1795.

By Major TENCH, of the Marines,

LATE OF HIS MAJESTY'S SHIP ALEXANDER.

―――――――

LONDON:

PRINTED FOR J. JOHNSON, ST. PAUL'S CHURCH-YARD.

M.DCC.XCVI.

PREFACE.

THE following Letters were written under very adverfe circumftances, in a part of France remote from the beaten track in which travellers generally keep, and where curiofity has feldom led to obfervation. As connected with that ftupendous object, which has concentrated the attention not only of Europe, but of every quarter of this planet where human communications reach, they are offered to the Public. A con‑fiderable part of the collection was unavoid‑ably dedicated to matters which muft, from their nature, be uninterefting to a majority of readers; but the author trufts to the im‑

portance

portance of the ſubjeƈt to compenſate for the poverty of the relation. Since his return to England they have been reviſed; and would have been earlier ſent to the preſs, had not reaſons of a private nature interpoſed to pro-craſtinate his intention.

LETTERS

LETTER I.

MY DEAR FRIEND,   On board le Marat,
Breſt, 9th Nov. 1794.

A PERFORMANCE of thoſe flattering promiſes, which we exchanged at parting, to meet for a few days in London, about Chriſtmas next, provided the exigencies of ſervice would permit, muſt be ſuſpended for the preſent—to be fulfilled when—is one of thoſe ſecrets of f turity, which I dare not truſt my imagination to anticipate.

The wayward fortune of your friend has again* expoſed him to be taken by the " inſolent foe," after an unſuccefsful, but I truſt not inglorious combat, againſt very ſuperior force. This diſaſtrous event happened on the 6th inſtant. †——

To

* The writer was taken priſoner in the laſt war in America.

† Here followed a minute relation of the battle, which the Alexander ſuſtained for two hours and a quarter, againſt

B   three

To our great furprize, the enemy's fhips continued to fire upon us after our colours were
ftruck. At firft we conceived, that this unpro-
voked prolongation of hoftilities arofe from their
not feeing that we had furrendered; but when
their knowledge of this event could no longer
be doubted, and the firing did not ceafe, fome
among us, joining to this conduct a recollection
of the decree of the convention, which forbade
quarter to be extended to Englifhmen, were almoft ready to believe, that it was defigned to be

three fhips, each of her own ftrength, and juft before fhe
ftruck againft *five*. But as all the circumftances of the
action, and of the caufes which led to it, have been detailed
by him, who like Cæfar, knew not only how to execute, but
to narrate deeds of glory, I have thought it right to fupprefs
my defcription; and beg leave to refer the reader to the official letter of Captain, now Rear Admiral Bligh, which appeared in the Gazette, either about the latter end of January, or the beginning of February, 1795.—The names
and force of the fquadron by which we were taken, were as
follows, under the command of Contre-Amiral Neilly.

	Guns.			Guns.
Le Tigre, - -	74	La Fraternité,	- -	40
Les Droits de l'Homme,	74	La Gentille,	- -	40
Le Jean Bart, - -	74	La Charente,	- -	40
Le Pelletier, - -	74	Le Papillon,	- -	14
Le Marat, - -	74			

executed

executed upon *us*; and fo irritated were our feamen, by this apparently wanton continuation of
attack, that they had once nearly determined to
renew the fight, and fell their lives as dearly
as poffible. At length, however, their firing
ceafed.

Knowing from fad experience, that in fuch a
fituation all diftinction of property is confounded,
and that the officers and public ftores of the fhip
become at once the indifcriminate prey of the
enemy and their own crew, I left the deck, and
defcended into the bread-room. There I had in
the morning depofited one of my trunks, out of
which I filled a clothes bag with fuch neceffaries
as I thought would be moft ufeful to me, and
left it in the charge of my fervant, while I endeavoured to fave a part of what a very large
trunk, lodged in the marine ftore-room, contained. But this refolution I was incapable of effect-
ing. The cock-pit, which I was obliged to pafs
through, prefented fuch a fcene of mifery, as ba-
nifhed every feeling, but forrow and pity. I found
myfelf encompaffed at once by the dead and the
dying. The groans of the latter, joined to the
cries of the wounded, on whom operations were

performing

performing by the furgeon, and to the blood which overflowed my feet, filled me with horror and difguft.

> " Sight fo deform what heart of rock could long
> " Dry-ey'd behold?"———— MILTON.

It " quelled my beft of man;" and, after two ineffectual attempts to penetrate acrofs this ftage of woe, I returned to my fervant, and made a few farther arrangements of what was left to me.

By this time the French boats had boarded us, and taken poffeffion of the fhip. When I attempted to afcend to the deck, I found every hatchway guarded by French fentinels, who re-fufed to let me pafs. In vain did I expoftulate with them; all the anfwer I could obtain was, " *Citoyen, tels font mes ordres. Je fuis républicain!*" At length I faw a French officer, and begged his interference, which, after fome hefitation, was granted, and on his fpeaking to the fen-tinel, I was fuffered to proceed to the deck, where I found all that confufion and diforder reigning which I had expected. The Admiral had, I learned, been already fent away. I en-
quired

quired for the French commanding officer, and
was directed to a refpectable looking old man,
to whom I prefented my fword, telling him, at
the fame time, that I hoped, and trufted, we
fhould be allowed to retain our private property, and be protected from pillage. He anfwered me, that we certainly fhould. I had,
however, but juft turned from him, when a
French officer feized on my crofs-belt, and de-
manded it. On my refufing to comply with
this mandate, he faid it was arms; which I denied, and bade him, if he thought I had not
made a full furrender of thofe, to fearch me.
To all the arguments and proteftations which
I could ufe, this gentleman thought proper to
anfwer by force only; fo that, finding farther
refiftance vain, I yielded up the belt to him,
when his motive for divefting me of this dangerous implement of war, at once appeared—
a large filver plate, which was attached to it,
being the bait. This he very compofedly
took off and put in his pocket, trailing the
belt carelefsly along after him as he marched
away.

The commanding officer being extremely

urgent that we fhould quit the fhip directly, I got leave to make another effort to recover fome more of my effects; but univerfal plunder and uproar had now taken place. The ftore-rooms and cabins were broken open and pillaged, and the moft brutal exceffes committed. I was furprized to find the French feamen and foldiers even more forward than our own, in fearching for wine and fpirits, and equally eager to intoxicate themfelves: a new trait in their national character.

About four o'clock I quitted the Alexander, carrying with me my bag, which was all I had been able to fave, and was conducted, with feveral other officers, on board Le Marat, a name of ill omen, and not too predictive, thought I, when I heard it proclaimed, of the virtues of humanity and generofity. Here I found our gallant and refpected commander, who introduced me to Captain Le Franq, the commander of the fhip, by whom I was civilly received. This gentleman fpeaks very good Englifh, which he learned in the laft war, when he was a prifoner in England and in the Eaft Indies. In a very candid manner, he repeatedly defired us not to be
under

under any apprehenſions about the treatment
which we were to receive; for that if he, or any
of his officers or men, ſhould be found guilty
of ill uſing priſoners of war, the republic would
puniſh the offenders. When we complained to
him of having been plundered, he proteſted,
that he had given the ſtricteſt orders to forbid it
to thoſe who had boarded us; and that he was
ſure they could not be the authors of our loſſes,
as his officers were all *gentlemen* (he ſpoke in
Engliſh) and his men in a ſtate of the moſt ex-
emplary diſcipline. We anſwered, that among
the great number of boats which had boarded the
Alexander, from every ſhip in the ſquadron, it
was impoſſible for ſtrangers to point out either the
names or the perſons, or the ſhips to which the
parties might belong; and that we chiefly attributed our loſſes to the precipitancy by which
we had been compelled to quit our own ſhip.
Upon hearing this, Captain Le Franq very fairly
and honourably propoſed, that one of ourſelves
ſhould be ſelected, and ſent on board the Alexander, in order to bring away whatever could be
found belonging to any of us. We thanked him
for his offer, and embraced it; but the officer

who went on this fervice was able to obtain very little. Some few articles, indeed, he *did* recover; and to-day, as many more of us as chofe to go again on a fimilar errand, were permitted, and French officers were fent with us, to enforce the order for a fearch: it was conducted in a very open and liberal manner, although it ended almoft as fruitlefsly as the former, the poffeffors of their newly-acquired property having taken effectual means to fecrete nine parts in ten of it from our fcrutiny. My large trunk, however, I difcovered, clofe to the door of the ftore-room, wherein it had been depofited. I bleffed my good fortune, and fprang to it: but what was my mortification, to find, that of all its former treafures (having clofely packed it with my moft valuable articles) nothing remained but two bits of black ribbon, ferving to faften my gorget!

We had been more than two hours in Captain Le Franq's cabin, without having had any re-frefhment offered to us, when, at about fix o'clock, fupper was announced. The captain, inviting Admiral Bligh, and all of us, to follow him, led us into the ward-room, where we found the banquet fpread, and all the officers of the

etat-

etat-major, or ward-room mefs, affembled. I
was no ftranger (as you know) to the cuftoms
of the French on land, which were never re-
markable for delicacy and cleanlinefs; but I had
never before feen their mode of living on board
their fhips of war. Our entertainment was ferved
up on a large clumfy deal table, which was placed
(to fpeak in fea-language) not fore and aft, but
athwart fhip, very awkwardly and inconveniently,
furrounded by benches and lockers, and in place
of a table-cloth was covered by a piece of green
painted canvas. Sweet are the joys of hunger,
on fuch an occafion! After a faft of thirteen
hours, and that in a day of fuch unceafing agitation as we had paffed, neither this circumftance,
nor the garlic with which the meat abounded;
nor a want of knives and forks, and a change of
plates; nor the battling of the *mouffes* (dirty
ragged cabin-boys) for the fcraps which were left;
nor the appearance of the company, who all fat
with their hats, or red caps, on; nor their vociferation of the word *Citoyen*, the only title they
ufed in pledging each other to republican toafts,
could prevent me from making a moft fatisfactory
repaft. Nothing fhort of the evidence of my
fenfes

fenfes could, neverthelefs, have made me believe,
that fo much filthinefs could be quietly fubmitted
to, when it might be fo eafily prevented. Indeed,
a fhip is in all fituations very unfavourable to
fcrupulous nicety; but no defcription can convey
an adequate idea to a Britifh naval officer, who
has not witneffed it, of the grofs and polluted
ftate in which the French habitually keep all
parts of their veffels, if I may judge from what
I fee in this. And to complete the jeft, Captain
Le Franq has more than once boafted to us of
the fuperior attention which he pays to the cleanlinefs of his fhip.

In the courfe of our converfation at fupper,
we learned, that this fquadron had been purpofely difpatched from Breft, to intercept us on
our outward bound paffage, being furnifhed with
exact intelligence of the time we had put into
Plymouth, and of our force and deftination*.

But

* The Alexander failed from Portfmouth on the 13th of
September, having under her command the Canada of 74
guns, the Adamant of 50, the Thorn floop, and a convoy
bound to the Mediterranean. Owing to foul winds we put
into Plymouth on the 16th, whence we failed on the 26th
of

But to proceed with the adventures of your friend in a regular detail. After supper, Admiral Bligh, and those officers who had saved their beds, went up into the cabin, where places to sleep in were allotted to them, while a sail was spread below, for the majority who had lost their's, in which number I was included. This humble couch, which was as good as circumstances would allow our hosts to furnish, or as we could reasonably expect, would have been perfectly satisfactory to us, had we been permitted to retire to it. But our entertainers, no longer checked by the presence of their chief, who had retired, and

of the same month. The Adamant and Thorn, with the merchant ships, parted from us off Cape St. Vincent. The Canada was in company when we were chased, saw us engage, and strike. Her signal was made, to join and suppor, us; but this, which she attempted, a manœuvre of the enemy prevented her from executing: Captain Hamilton, who commanded her, then very properly began his retreat. Malevolence was not wanting to attack his character upon this occasion; but I am happy in bearing my testimony, that farther perseverance on his side was not wished by us, as it would have caused only an useless effusion of blood, and the capture of two British ships of the line, instead of one.

elated by victory, and by an anticipation of the
triumph which awaited them at Breft, on the
novel and glorious atchievement of capturing a
Britifh 74 gun fhip, now called for a frefh fupply
of wine, and began to fing, in a loud key, republican fongs, which were interrupted only by
queftions to us, that delicacy fhould have with-
holden them from afking.   One of them, taking
a candle in his hand, begged me to look at two
prints of heads, as large as life, of Pelletier and
Marat, " Ah !" faid he, pointing to the latter,
" behold the friend of the people ! he who fhed
" his blood for them !"   I looked, as he had
defired me, and thought I faw all the diabolical
qualities, by which that monfter was marked in
his life-time, depicted in this portrait.   Prudence, however, kept me filent.   Poor Pelletier
came in for no fhare of this gentleman's eulogy ;
and as to Robefpierre, they all fpoke of him, and
" his reign," with great bitternefs and detefta-
tion.

We were compelled to rife at a very early
hour next morning, the fail on which we had
flept being wanted.   I would willingly have
walked on the quarter-deck, according to the
Englifh

English cuſtom; but it was ſo crowded by the
men, and ſo greaſy and ſlippery, that I found it
impracticable. The captain, overhearing us talk
on this ſubject, very gravely ſaid, that he never
allowed his people to eat between decks, but
always made them do ſo upon deck, *in order to
keep his ſhip clean*. When we ſaw that after theſe
meals they neither ſcraped nor waſhed the decks,
we were at no loſs to account for the ſtate in
which we found them; and no doubt thoſe whom
it profeſſionally concerned, duly noted this curious improvement in the œconomy of a ſhip
of war.

About eight o'clock the boatſwain and his
mates went to the different hatchways of the
ſhip, and ſummoned the crew in a loud voice,
" *aux prières.*" My ignorance of what theſe
prayers might be, did not long continue. The
quarter-deck was immediately thronged by men
and officers, who with united voice ſang the
Marſeilles Hymn, with a fervor and enthuſiaſm
of manner which aſtoniſhed me. I had heard
it at a diſtance on the preceding evening; and
upon enquiry learned, that it was thus publickly
performed twice a day, by order of the government.

ment. The fublime mufic of this fine lyric compofition, the gaiety breathed by the *Carmagnole,*
and by many other popular airs which are continually in their mouths, during their moft ordinary
occupations, muft produce a prodigious effect on
the pliant minds of Frenchmen, and highly contribute to invigorate that fpirit of idolatry for a
republic, and that hatred and contempt of monarchy, which it is fo much the intereft of their
leaders to encourage. I need not point out to
you the good policy of fuch national eftablifh-
ments, and how deep a knowledge of human
nature they manifeft; perhaps no other country
is fo culpably indifferent to the foundation of
fimilar inftitutions as our own. We fire, indeed,
a few lazy guns on the anniverfaries of the King's
birth, acceffion, and other fimilar occafions; but
we never ftimulate the paffions of our foldiery,
by recalling to their memories, in periodic exhibitions, the days on which their forefathers won
the fields of Agincourt, Blenheim, and Minden;
nor re-animate the ardent energy of our feamen,
by public recitals of the victories of a Ruffel, a
Hawke, a Rodney, and a Howe. And yet the
hiftories of the greateft nations, both ancient and

9   modern,

modern, sufficiently demonstrate the power of such exhibitions over the human mind ; and justify me in affirming, that no people ever rose to superlative dominion who did not employ them. How would the flame of heroism be enkindled in our youth, on hearing these celebrations performed by the veterans of Chelsea and Greenwich ! And what still more important sentiments would be diffused through the mass of our people, if they were frequently reminded of those glorious æras, when John was compelled to sign Magna Charta; and when the declaration of the rights of the people was made the foundation of William's throne !

This digression towards a country, which busy remembrance points to with unceasing anxiety, could not be suppressed. To proceed with my observations here :—The republican spirit is inculcated not in songs only, for in every part of the ship I find emblems purposely displayed to awaken it. All the orders relating to the discipline of the crew are hung up, and prefaced by the words *Liberté, Egalité, Fraternité, ou la Mort*, written in capital letters. The *bonnet rouge*, or cap of liberty, is erected in several places, and

crowns

crowns the figure on the prow of the ſhip, which repreſents the demagogue whoſe name ſhe bears, and on which is written an extract from the declaration of the rights of man.   In the cabin (to which the officers are entitled to reſort at all times) *Liberté & Egalité* are pourtrayed in female characters, the former brandiſhing a ſword, and the latter nurſing a numerous offspring, with impartial attention to the wants of all. But a picture of another ſort alſo caught my eye : it was paſted on the *outſide* of a door, which led to the apartment of an officer, and repreſented the prime miniſter of Great Britain conducting to a *guillotine* his blindfolded ſovereign.   The perſon to whom it belonged, on ſeeing me regard it with mingled indignation and contempt, would have begun a converſation on the ſubject, had I not prevented him by turning my back and walking away.   Indeed, next to the poor emigrants, Mr. Pitt, or " *Miniſtre Peet*," as they always call him, ſeems to be the primary object of their abhorrence. Hated name ! never breathed but in curſes, never coupled but with execrations ! To hear them, one would ſuppoſe that he is the only man in England hoſtile to their growing republic. Even
Captain

Captain Le Franq, who has certainly hitherto
behaved towards us with more delicacy than the
other officers, did not fcruple to call him " a
" Robefpierre." To argue with thefe people I
find impoffible; " but to be grave exceeds all
" power of face." My only refource, on fuch
occafions, is to afk fome queflion foreign to the
fubject they wifh to talk upon : even here I can
make no progrefs; I am either repulfed by want
of common knowledge; or bewildered in contra-
diction. Having eftablifhed it as a maxim, that
fome degree of information may always be gained by talking to men of their own profeffions, I
am as inquifitive as I modeftly can be, about
their naval inftitutions. But, if my queftion be
heard by more than one, fuch fhocking abrupt
oppofitions of opinion follow, and fo pertina-
cioufly does each party defend his affertion on the
moft ordinary points, that my only alternative, to
prevent a perfect equilibrium of mind, is to
place the little confidence left at my difpofal in
the champion who has been leaft violent and vo-
ciferous; agreeably to the old obfervation, which
fays, the ftill ftream is the deepeft. Their ignorance, indeed, upon almoft every fubject which

C   has

has been stated, is deplorable. One of them, in
pure simplicity of heart, asked me if London
were as large as Brest ? I was contented to answer him, by saying I had never seen Brest. He
was greatly surprized, on being informed that
London is a sea-port; and, to recompense me for
my intelligence, told me Paris did not enjoy
that advantage, as he had heard, for he confessed
he had never been there. A second had read
Shakespeare, " and did not like him; he was
" too *sombre*."—" Pray, sir, do you allude to any
" particular play ?" He seemed confounded; but,
after some hesitation, said, " Yes, to *Paucippe*."—
" To Paucippe !" exclaimed I; " you mistake
" the name, there is not any of his plays which
" bears such a title." He was confident he was
right, and therefore I begged to know the fable
of the piece, or the names of the other characters; but with them, this critical reader did
not pretend to any acquaintance. I need not observe to you, that none of these officers had ever
served in the navy of France, but in the most
subordinate capacities, under the king's government, except the captain, who had commanded
a cutter under Monsieur de Suffrein, but who
had

had neverthelefs been bred up in the fervice of the Eaft India company.

We anchored in Breft-Water about three o'clock this morning, and I prefume to hope we fhall very foon be fent on fhore ; but whether, or not, on parole, does not feem quite clear. They an-fwer with great ambiguity, and apparent unwil-lingnefs, to all queftions on this head, pretending that they are ignorant of what is cuftomary, but afluring us that we fhall be treated well. To be fhut up in a prifon, in this cold and dreary feafon that is coming on, is what I dread to look forward to. We frequently defcribe to them the parole which is allowed to all French officers in England. But, whatever is to be our lot, I fhall not wonder at their taking almoft any ftep to rid themfelves of fo numerous a troop of in-truders on their fociety and table. Their own mefs confifts of fixteen perfons, befides the cap-tain, who lives in common with his officers, al-though this affociation, they tell me, is forbidden in their naval inftructions ; but it feems thefe little deviations are winked at, in certain cafes, to prevent the too weighty tax of a feparate table. We breakfaft every morning at nine o'clock on

Gloucefter

Gloucester cheese (taken out of an Fnglifh prize)
good brown bread, called *pain d egalité*, which
they bake on board, and a thin acid claret, of
which the Frenchmen drink very liberally. This
does not feem to argue the fcarcity of flour
among them, which has been fo much infifted
upon in England. A hint of this was dropped,
and great derifion followed, on their part, at the
idea of ftarving fuch a country as France, by
cutting off a few cafual fupplies by fea. We
dine between twelve and one, and fup between
fix and feven o'clock. On all thefe occafions
there is a fufficient quantity of provifions provided, though the dirty ftate in which it is ferved
up, would difguft a Hottentot. I have mentioned before, that during our meals we are furrounded by filthy ragged cabin-boys, whofe appearance, contentions and impertinence, are in-
tolerable. Among this crew of little blackguards,
two were pointed out to me as the fon and
nephew of *Delcher*, who is one of the reprefentatives from the Weftern Pyrenees to the convention. It is certain, that when I challenged
the boys with it, they confirmed it to me, and
feemed to glory in their fituation. I was alfo

fhown

ſhown a third boy, about eleven years old, who
is the ſon of an *emigrated nobleman.* In him,
nature is not quite ſubdued: " *Le petit* ———
" *pleure quelquefois,*" ſaid one of the lieutenants
to me.

I have forgotten to mention before, that on
the day of our being brought on board the
Marat, we were ſhown their furnace (which is
the oven) for heating ſhot. It is well contrived,
and the balls, by means of a pair of bellows,
would ſoon be made red-hot; but I doubt not
that " even-handed juſtice" will oftener render
this dreadful implement of deſtruction, like
" the ingredients of the poiſoned chalice, rather
" the plague of the inventor," than the deſtroyer
of the objects of its vengeance. The motion
of a ſhip at ſea muſt, I apprehend, not only
cauſe its effect to be very precarious, but its
uſe very dangerous. Be this as it may, every
thing here was prepared, the faggots were laid,
and the ſhot were placed between them; and
they aſſured us, that in the moment we had
ſtruck, they were juſt going to heat them for
us: a confeſſion which, conſidering the odds
that we had fought againſt, was not very ho-

nourable

nourable to republican gallantry. All their
ſhips of war, they told us, were provided with
ſimilar furnaces.

In the little time I have been in my new ſituation, nothing has ſurprized me more than the
quantity of Engliſh articles I every where ob-
ſerve. The cheeſe, as I ſaid before, was *Glou-
ceſter*; to which I might have added, that the
plates it was ſerved upon were *Stafford*, and the
knives it was cut by were *Sheffield*, while the
coats, hats, and ſhoes of thoſe who were eating
it, were alſo chiefly of Britiſh manufactures.
" *Prize, prize*," is the only anſwer we receive
to our enquiries. Surely what one of their officers told me cannot be true! Seeing me juſt
now looking up one of the arms which help
to form this capacious port, and which is
crowded with ſhipping, he aſſured me that
they were all Engliſh, and not leſs than 400
in number. It is too well aſcertained, that
the French have been, during the preſent war,
wonderfully ſuccefsful againſt our trading veſ-
ſels. Their frigates, I am informed, cruize in
ſmall detached ſquadrons to the weſtward of
Europe; whilſt we confine ours almoſt totally
to

to the Channel, which I prefume to confider a
very injudicious difpofition of them, in a war
wherein the enemy have no privateers, and
when confequently the little ports on the French
coaft, within Ufhant, fhould be lefs objects of
our jealoufy than heretofore. Provided our
grand fleet can, after a parade off Breft, return
into Spithead or Torbay, without being mate-
rially damaged by the weather, we feem to be
fatisfied, and conclude that all is going on well
on the waters.

How I fhall be able to procure money for
bills on London, during my probable term of
refidence in this country, is not the fmalleft of
my inquietudes. I have hinted the difficulty to
Captain Le Franq; but from his real or af-
fumed ignorance, one might be led to fuppofe,
that paper-money had always been the only
currency of France. The little cafh I had by
me, I took care to fecure in my pocket, which
efcaped unfearched. It is, however, very inadequate to adminifter to my wants, ftripped as
I am almoft to my laft fhirt. Small as it is,
fomething like an attack was made upon it juft
now. An old *militaire,* who is captain of the

C 4   troops

troops on board, came to me, and, with many
profeſſions of eſteem, offered to ſerve me, by
giving me, in exchange for Engliſh guineas,
twenty-four livres in paper, each; aſſuring me
that I ſhould ſubject myſelf to diſagreeable con-
ſequences, by offering to purchaſe with gold,
when I might land. He brought the *aſſignats*
in his hand to tempt me: but I begged leave,
with a profuſion of compliments, to decline
this courteous propoſal. Surely gold and *aſſignats* cannot be deemed by all Frenchmen of
equal value! *Nous verrons!* At preſent all is
myſtery to me.—This ſaid captain has a ſon on
board, a fine youth, who is a corporal in his
father's company.

Admiral Bligh is gone on ſhore to-day with
the French captain, in order to be taken before
the repreſentatives on miſſion here. He will
probably gain ſome intelligence of what we are
deſtined to, and we expect his return with impatience. We are too well acquainted with his
feelings and ſentiments, to doubt that he will
heſitate to ſacrifice even his own perſonal comforts to promote ours, and to prevent our being
ſeparated from him.

Upon

Upon furrendering our fwords we were given
to underftand, that they fhould be reftored to us,
agreeably to the ufages of war among civilized
nations, but nothing has been lately faid of this
reftitution ; and the French officers, on being
afked about it, only fhake their heads, and plead
ignorance.—How unlike the polifhed generofity
which once diftinguifhed Frenchmen towards
enemies, who, in fubmitting to the imperious
neceffity of war, yielded up arms without a ftain!
——Adieu !

LETTER

LETTER II.

Normandie, prifon-fhip, in
Breft-Water, 1ft Dec. 1794.

I MUST continue to write on to you, as if I
had the means of regularly tranfmitting my
letters. In the horrid dungeon in which I am
now immured, it forms my only confolation
to talk to you, although you cannot hear me;
and to complain to you, although you cannot
fuccour me.

Two days after the date of my firft letter, we
were all, except Admiral Bligh, fent from Le
Marat, on board this prifon-fhip. Such a change
did not much furprize us; for the reception
which the Admiral experienced from the reprefentatives, was fo cold and myfterious, as to afford neither intelligence nor confolation; and
Le Franq, who was his introducer and interpreter, affected utter ignorance of their intentions towards us.

Our fituation here is extremely irkfome. The
captain of the veffel and his lieutenants are men

3   of

of ferocious manners and brutal behaviour, high-
flying patriots, whofe fupreme delight confifts in
blafpheming all revealed religion, and in abufing
the Englifh nation.   In the day-time we have
nominally the liberty of walking upon the deck;
but this privilege is frequently fo curtailed, by
the caprices of our gaolers, as to amount almoft to a prohibition.   At night we are crowded
into a fmall cabin, and hardly allowed light
enough to undrefs ourfelves by.   Luckily, however, I have recovered my mattrefs and a couple
of blankets.   We eat with the officers of the
fhip, who are allowed a *traitement,* or table-
money, of three livres fix fols a day, befides a
ration of provifions, for each of us; fo that the
fault does not feem to be imputable to the government.   But either the markets of Breft are
extravagantly dear, or thefe patriotic gentlemen
make an advantage of us; for hardly a day paffes
in which we have a fufficiency of any thing but
coarfe brown, or rather black, bread, fo full of
fandy particles as to be almoft uneatable.   Our
breakfaft at firft was bread and butter, and a
fmall red wine; but of late the butter has been
taken away, and either Newfoundland falt-fifh,

or

or falt herrings, fubftituted in its place. Thefe, indeed, are petty grievances, which would be eafily
tolerated, were they not inceffantly aggravated by
the difagreeable tempers, and debafed fentiments,
of thofe with whom we are obliged to live and
converfe. We are furrounded by American veffels, but cannot hold with any of them the fmalleft
communication. A hope of hearing from England, or of conveying aught to it, muft not be
indulged. We have been told, that if we choofe
to venture the experiment of fending open letters
by the poft through Switzerland, we may do it;
but that they muft be firft taken to the reprefentatives, who will order them to be read, and
forward them, if they contain information of a
private nature only. This precaution is reafonable enough; but I have been affured by an
officer of the fhip, who is in a civil capacity,
that I may fpare myfelf the trouble of fending
any, for that to his knowledge they are always
thrown afide, and forgotten, in the office to
which they are carried. The number of prifoners
on board is about four hundred, nearly all of
whom are Englifh; and three more veffels ap-
propriated

propriated to a fimilar ufe, which alfo feem
quite full, are moored clofe to us. On the return of fome frigates from a cruize, a few days
fince, we received an acceffion to our number
which furprized me :—twenty emigrants—who
for the crime of being Englifhmen were taken
out of an *American* fhip at fea, after which the
veffel was fuffered to proceed on her voyage to
Philadelphia, and the reft of the cargo remained
unmolefted.

I find that I acted prudently in not parting
with my guineas. Since I have been here, my
brother-officer from Le Marat has honoured
me by a fecond vifit, and offered *thirty* livres
for a guinea, pointing out one of the ferjeants of
the guard, through whom the bufinefs might at
any time be tranfacted. I again begged permiffion
to decline this benevolent gentleman's propofal,
and alfo two others of a fimilar tendency, which
were made to me here. Nor did the event de-
ceive my expectation; for to day a little Jew,
who mounts a cockade, and belongs to a frigate
in the harbour, came on board, and fecretly
gave me two hundred and fifty livres for five
guineas, declaring it to be the market price
on

on fhore. What think you of thefe fpecimens
of republican honour and delicacy to children
of misfortune, like us? I was fo tranfported by
indignation at thofe who had thus endeavoured
to cheat me, that I could not help afking them,
on their attempting to renew the fubject, if the
law did not forbid the depreciation of paper,
when bartered for gold. This regulation, they
pretend, relates to French gold only. To exchange a *louis* for more than its nominal value
in *affignats* were criminal : but mark the curious
diftinction! An Englifh guinea, and a Portugueze johannes, are articles of merchandize,
whofe worth depends on the election of the
buyer. Well! I have yet four Englifh guineas
left! Let me look at them! Oh " ye ever-
" young, loved, and delicate wooers! whofe
" blufh doth thaw the confecrated fnow on
" Dian's lap;"—and before whom even the
fternnefs of modern republican virtue melts
into thin air, — tenacioufly will I treafure ye
up!——Adieu!

LETTER

LETTER III.

Normandie, prifon-fhip, Breft
Water, 7th Dec. 1794.

ADMIRAL BLIGH has been allowed to vifit
us twice or thrice fince our feparation
took place.   He ftill remains on board Le
Marat, with his fon, a little boy of ten years
old, and two young midfhipmen, who are alfo
permitted to be with him.   Until this day he
has been unable to give us any information,
and was even ignorant of what was to be his
own lot.   He is now promifed to be fent, on his
parole, to Quimper, in Bretagne; and in addition to innumerable proofs of kindnefs and
regard, which I have experienced from him
ever fince I have been under his command, he
has honoured me by obtaining leave for me
to accompany him, as his *aid de-camp and interpreter.*   Since my laft letter he has been on
board *La Montagne,* to fee Vice Admiral Villaret de Joyeufe, the commander in chief of the
fleet here, and who acted in that capacity againft
Lord

Lord Howe on the firft of June. He told me
that he was very politely received, and was preffed
to accept of pecuniary affiftance, which he declined; but Admiral Villaret plainly hinted to
him, that he was obliged to fupprefs much
of the regard which he willed to fhow to
him, from the delicacy of his fituation, in the
prefent temper of the times. Monfieur Renaudin, late commander of the *Vengeur*, who
was taken, after the finking of his fhip, on the
firft of June, and is juft returned from England, has vifited him on board Le Marat. This
gentleman declares, in loud terms, the humanity of the Englifh, and the polite attentions he
received from many of our moft diftinguifhed
naval officers, whofe generofity left him no
want: Of this lift I remember the names of
Lord Howe, Admiral M'Bride, Captain Ben-
tinck, and Captain Schomberg. Monfieur Renaudin alfo made a tender of his purfe to Admiral Bligh; but I have reafon to believe, that
it was not done with that explicit franknefs,
which could hope to fuperfede the offer of
Monfieur Villaret, even had it been made previoufly to it. By the way, the re-appearance

of

of Renaudin, does not a little aftonifh the
French; for the convention, in order to gratify
the national 'vanity, and inflame the minds of
the people againft the Englifh, had publickly
announced, that Le Vengeur, with *all her crew,*
funk with colours flying, difdaiming to accept
of quarter from flaves whom they defpifed;
and a decree was even paffed, to perpetuate
this heroic refolution, by erecting a monument
to the memory of the event.

I am forry to fay, that Monfieur Renaudin
echoed the profeffion of his commander in
chief, in lamenting that the political prejudices
which reign here will prevent him alfo from
acting up to the extent of his wifhes, in attending to the Englifh, and the Admiral in particular. What evils do not thefe political phren-
zies generate? Be this as it may, I am all alive
at the thought of the fcene about to burft upon
me; and there are moments when I am almoft
tempted not to regret a captivity, which opens
an inlet into this extraordinary country at fuch
a period as the prefent; but thefe momentary
illufions flit before the memory of the fcenes
I have left behind. Can curiofity, all-powerful

D   as

as it is, ſtand in oppoſition to love and friend-
ſhip? Let me, however, but quit La Normandie, and then we will ſtrike the balance.
To-morrow I am to bid adieu to her darkſome
round: how joyfully! And yet I ſhall not leave
without a tear of commiſeration thoſe gallant
comrades, with whom I have ſo lately fought,
and ſo ſeverely ſuffered.

The few remarks I have been able to make
are entirely nautical. I ſhall detail them to you
when I can reviſe them at my leiſure at
Quimper. From a fear of being ſearched, I
have uſed ſome extraordinary precautions to
ſecure them; and if they be found they will
not be eaſily underſtood, for I have ſo tranſ-
poſed the natural order of the ſentences, and
ſo intermixed words from all the languages
which I could recollect (not excepting that of
New Holland) that it would puzzle the interpreter of the convention to decypher them.——
Adieu.

LETTER

LETTER IV.

Le Marat, Breft-Water,
15th Dec. 1794.

THAT leifure which I fo lately looked forward to at Quimper, feems likely to be afforded to me here. I was removed from the prifon-fhip on the 8th inftant, and allowed to bring my fervant with me, expecting to be fent immediately on parole; but this event, like the refolutions of the Dutch councils, feems to be put off *ad referendum*. We receive daily affurances that it is to take place, and are daily difappointed of feeing it arrive. I enjoy, however, the fociety and converfation of the Admiral; and as he does not fpeak French, I am the chief medium through which he communicates with thofe who furround him, Captain Le Franq, who is married, living almoft entirely on fhore. So that here I remain, with nothing to do but to afk and anfwer queftions from morning to night. Thefe are chiefly nautical; and as you know my fentiments on

D 2   the

the confequence of all naval concerns to Englifhmen, I am induced to believe you will
concur with me in thinking the fubject momentous, however trite the remarks, or unim-
portant the obfervations of your correfpondent
may prove.

Whether Selden's affertion, that " we have an
" hereditary uninterrupted right to the fove-
" reignty of our feas, conveyed to us from our
" earlieft anceftors, in truft for our lateft pof-
" terity," be perfectly deducible either from
the nature of things, or from the authority of
hiftory, I fhall not ftay to enquire. But I will
venture to affirm, that when we fuffer this right,
however acquired, to depart from us, the fun
of England may be truly faid to be fet for
ever.

When the queftion of the relative naval
ftrength of the two nations is agitated, which
it often is, I am tempted to cry out to my
country, in the words of the Grecian oracle, —
" Truft to your wooden walls."—I am the more
confirmed in this opinion, from reading every
day in the *bulletins* of the aftonifhing fuc-
ceffes of this people, both in the Pyrenees, and

on

on the frontier of Holland. They openly boaſt
of being able, in a ſhort time, to penetrate to
Madrid; to force the German powers to peace;
and to totally ſubdue the Dutch.—And then
" Delenda eſt Carthago." I accuſe not thoſe
with whom I converſe of uſing this, or any
other Latin phraſe; but you will ſmile on being
told that they habitually call us Carthaginians,
and themſelves Romans. They pay us, however, the compliment of declaring, that we
are the only enemies worth combating. They
ſtigmatize the Spaniards as cowards: at German tactics, when oppoſed to the energy and
enthuſiaſm of republicans, they laugh: Dutch
apathy can alarm no one. But this reſpect is
confined to our naval character. Our impo-
tent interference and puny attempts on the Con-
tinent they treat only with ridicule and deriſion.
This ſpirit is not new: A noble lord, now high
in rank in the Britiſh army, told me nearly
twenty years ago, when we were on ſervice together in America, that when he was very
young, and travelling in France, a general officer, on hearing him relate that he was de-
ſigned for the army, expreſſed his ſurprize that
any

any Englifhman, to whom the choice was left,
fhould hefitate to prefer entering into the navy.
Are the fcorn and contempt of our enemies
neceffary to teach us in what our true grandeur, our real national pre-eminence, confifts? It is certain that at prefent we far furpafs
them in the number of our fhips, in the dex-
terity of our feamen, and in the interior regulations of our fervice; but I am perfuaded,
that they will hereafter ftrain every nerve to
equal and exceed us. I know, that by very high
authority the naval power of France has been
denominated " forced and unnatural;" but let
thofe who apply to it epithets fo devoid of
knowledge and reflection, remember the fhort
period in which Louis XIV. created this navy,
and its refurrection in 1778, when, to the
aftonifhment of all Europe, notwithftanding its
wafted and difaftrous condition but fifteen years
before, it fuddenly ftarted up, fingly, to conteft
the empire of the fea with Britain, and for four
years (until the 12th of April 1782) poifed
the fcale of victory againft its formidable antagonift.

Nature has denied to France a port in the
Channel,

Channel, capable of receiving large fhips; but if art can fupply the deficiency, they feem determined to employ it to its utmoft extent. Whether the works at Cherbourg are proceeding or not, I cannot exactly learn; but it is certain, that the fcheme of rendering it fecure for line of battle fhips is not utterly abandoned; and who can doubt, that it will either be carried on there, or in fome neighbouring port, with accelerated vigour, on a return of peace ? Their warlike fpirit now runs fo high, and is fo univerfally diffufed, that many years muft elapfe ere it will fubfide. It is a train of gun-powder, to which, in the prefent temper of the people, a fpark will give fire. A hatred of England is foftered with unceafing care. In nothing does this inveterate fpirit againft us demonftrate itfelf fo bitterly, as in the abhorrence with which they always mention our taking poffeffion of Toulon: " You gained it like " traitors; you fled from it like poltroons." On the celebrated meafure of making them a prefent of four fhips of the line, and fix thoufand of their beft feamen, which were fent to Breft and Rochfort from the Mediterranean,

they

they often make themfelves merry, and us
ferious, by pointing out the fhips as they now
lie near to us, equipped and ready for fea ; and
by affirming, that the fupply of men thus received enabled them to fit out thofe cruizing
fquadrons which have fo forely diftreffed our
commerce.

How incumbent upon us, then, is it become
to guard againft the effects, which a propaga-
tion of this principle will inevitably produce!
Naval perfection is, I am well aware, like all
other perfections, placed beyond human reach ;
but the road to excellence is open.   In it we
have advanced before our rivals in all branches
of naval fuperiority but one: I mean fhip-
building.   Our veffels want length, and in the
conftruction of their bottoms are undeniably
very inferior to thofe of our enemies.   Hence
the continual efcapes of the French fleets from
ours, by fuperior failing, when we want to
bring them to action, which no fkill, diligence,
or bravery in our commanders can furmount.
We poffefs models from which we might learn
to correct our errors, and fupply our deficiencies ; but thefe patterns we are more ready
                                                      to

to deftroy than to imitate, as if fearful left com-
parifon of them with our own productions
fhould demonftrate our inferiority. Thus do
we continue obftinately to grope on in a dark
and fuperannuated track, merely becaufe our
anceftors preceded us in it. The truth is, the
art of fhip-building has been cultivated in
France by men of fcience, enlightened by a
previous ftudy of its theory : whereas in England it has been committed to the management
of thofe, who for the moft part have certainly
had no room to boaft of a fcientific education,
or a laborious examination of principles ; and
who could juftly lay claim to the merit of obfervation only. In a country fo eminent for
mathematical acquirements as ours, is it not extraordinary, that this moft ufeful branch of
knowledge fhould have been fo rarely applied
to national advantage ? What treatifes on this
important fubject can we oppofe to thofe, which
have been publifhed by French academicians,
and by Bouguier in particular ?

" Oh! for a bridge to pafs over two hundred
" thoufand *fans-culottes* !" I hear often exclaimed. Not that bridge which, according to Milton,

Death

Death confolidated acrofs Chaos, could be more
fatal to the remaining innocence of our firft
parents, than fuch a ftructure, in the fhape of
a fuperior fleet, would prove to their Englifh
defcendants. To prevent its erection, or to
have a chofen band of pioneers ready to deftroy
it, muft be our concern. I am, however, well
convinced, that hitherto they have never fe-
rioufly intended to invade us. This bug-bear
has now for more than a century been employed to affright us; to cramp our foreign
efforts; to diminifh our fum of productive la-
bour, one of the moft important of national
confiderations; and to debauch the manners of
our artifans and peafants in camps and bar-
racks *.

I have been curious to hear their account of
the fignal defeat, which they experienced on

* Since the above was written, I have read Major Cart-
wright's opinion on this fubject; and am only more
thoroughly convinced from his arguments, that neither a
" *Saxon militia*," or any other militia, beyond the regular
eftablifhment of the kingdom, is neceffary for our prefervation from invafion, which can be effected by a ftrong
naval force only.

the

the firft of June. This fhip was not in their
fleet, having been *launched fince*; but Captain
Le Franq commanded on that day L'Entre-
prenant, of 74 guns, and fome of the other officers were alfo parties concerned. Not the invincible fuperiority of Britifh feamen in fight-
ing and managing their fhips, but " Treafon!
" treafon! joined to the ignorance, obftinacy,
" and cowardice of Jean Bon St. André, caufed
" the lofs of the day." This naval dictator,
who from a Hugonot curate at the foot of the
Pyrenees was raifed to be a member of the
convention, and delegated by that body to fuperintend the equipment, and direct the manœuvres,
of a great fleet, is never mentioned but with
execration. His ftar fet with that of his mafter,
Robefpierre. I have heard an officer affert,
that he *faw* him, in the heat of the engagement, feized with a fudden emotion, ftart from
Admiral Villaret, near whom he was ftanding,
in the ftern-gallery of La Montagne, and run
pale and breathlefs down to the lower gun-
deck, under a pretence of encouraging the men;
nor could he be drawn thence, until the danger was over. " His feamanfhip," continued
this

this gentleman, " confifted in having made one
" fhort paffage. He might be a good *ecrivain*
" *ou fecretaire* ; but for the marine ! *Oh ! le*
" *vilain* ——— *!*" But for him, they fay, the
action would have been renewed, agreeably to
the wifhes and reprefentations of Monfieur Villaret ; for " *the Englifh were beaten, and might*
" *have been deftroyed.*"—I cannot help thinking,
that if *Jean Bon St. André* really did prevent a
renewal of the battle, he is not altogether fo ob-
noxious to the reproaches of his fellow-citizens
as they defcribe him to be. France is not the
firft republic which has profited, by declining to
combat a victorious enemy.—A fecond caufe
of the difafter of the day arofe from Lord
Howe having gained poffeffion of a copy of
the French fignals, which was procured by
" the guineas of Pitt ;" fo that he was enabled
to divine all their intentions, and to counteract
them. It is certain, that fome of their captains
were gullotined, after the return of the fleet to
Breft, but whether on a fufpicion of cowardice,
or perfidy, I know not. How confolatory to
French vanity are thefe fatisfactory folutions of
this dreadful overthrow ! Happy people ! who,

§   in

in all your conflicts againſt other nations, con-
quer by ſuperior ſkill and bravery only; and
are never vanquiſhed but by diſparity of number
on the ſide of your enemy, or by treachery
among yourſelves!

An error, which you with myſelf, and all other
Engliſhmen, have fallen into about this engagement, I muſt beg leave to correct, or at leaſt to
offer you my reaſons for believing it to be one.
—Lord Howe's account of the action ſtates, that
two ſhips of the enemy were ſunk. Of Le
Vengeur we will not ſpeak: here proof is poſi-
tive. But I am perſuaded ſhe was the only
one. This the French poſitively aſſert; and I
beg leave ſo far to join with them, as to ob-
ſerve, that when in Admiral Montagu's ſquadron (of which the Alexander formed a part)
we were chaſed, on the *ninth of June*, by the
ſhattered remnant of their fleet, which was
ſteering to Breſt, it was compoſed of *nineteen*
ſail of the line. Now, I apprehend it to be
certain, that on the day of battle this fleet con-
ſiſted but of twenty-ſix ſhips, *ſix* of which
were captured and brought into England; ſo
that it ſhould appear the *ſeventh*, Le Vengeur,
made up the original number. But beſide the

ſtrong

ftrong prefumption which this circumftance affords, I have received affurances from fo many
quarters (and particularly from one not remarkably friendly to the prefent fyftem) that
I am convinced one fhip only was fent to the
bottom on the firft of June. Indeed, in matters
of this nature, owing to the paffions of thofe
engaged, and the innumerable caufes which ob-
ftruct vifion, we fhould always receive fimilar
relations *cum grano falis*. In Lord Rodney's
action of the 12th of April 1782, a French
fhip, faid to be Le Diademe, was fuppofed to
be funk; but I believe fubfequent accounts
clearly evinced that fuch an event did not
happen. However, the French are more than
even with us upon this head; for I have heard
fome of them pofitively affirm, that they faw
three, and others four of our fhips, among
which was the Queen Charlotte, go down on
the firft of June. And when I affured the
gentleman who furnifhed me with this laft piece
of information, " on the evidence of his own
" fenfes," that he had been deceived, he only
fhook his head, and continued, like your friend,
a fceptic.

The remainder of this letter fhall be dedicated

cated to a detail of thofe detached parts of their
naval inftitutions, cuftoms, and prefent ftate,
which I have been enabled to pick up. In general I think them inferior, becaufe lefs eafily
practicable, to our own, but many of them deferve confideration. *" Fas eft et ab hofte doceri."*

The difcipline of their men ftruck me at the
firft view as contemptible; and yet I muft confefs that I was furprized by the ftate of fubor-
dination in which I afterwards found them. The
feaman or foldier addreffes his commander by
the title of *Citoyen*, and receives in return the
fame appellation; but in the five weeks I have
lived among them, I have witneffed only one
inftance of difobedience. The offender was a
foldier, who refufed to affift in performing fome
of the ordinary duties of the fhip. A court-mar-
tial, or *confeil de difcipline* as they call it, was immediately holden upon him, by order of Captain
Le Franq, who profecuted. It confifted of a
lieutenant of the fhip and three feamen, and of
two ferjeants and a corporal of the troops.
The prifoner pleaded ignorance of the law on
this head; and that when he had voluntarily
enrolled himfelf to ferve as a foldier, it was
under

under an idea of not being *compelled* to do that which *ought to be the result of inclination* only. This defence was deemed so unsatisfactory, that the offender was sentenced to three months imprisonment on shore.

All the judicial institutions of their navy, and the punishments allowed to be inflicted, as well as the cases to which they apply, are strictly defined. The *conseil de discipline* is impowered to try only inferior officers and men. The officers of the *état major* (answering nearly to those of our ward-room) and all above them, can be tried only by a board of officers, who assemble in the admiral's ship. Neither of these courts has the power of condemning to death: all offences of a capital nature must be tried before the revolutionary tribunal. The punishments enjoined are flogging in certain cases, the number of lashes being limited; running the gantlope; ducking from the yard-arm; confinement on shore, or in the lion's den (boatswain's storeroom); stoppage of pay; and degradation. The three last extend to officers. A prisoner's allowance of wine is always stopped. No man can be punished but by a sentence of the *conseil*
de

de difcipline; and, in carrying on the fervice of
the fhip, it is pofitively directed, that no
" French citizen" fhall, on any account whatever, be ftruck ; but he may be *pufhed* as vio-
lently as may be found neceffary. For giving
a box on the ear an officer would be cafhiered ;
but to dafh a man's head againft the fhip's fide,
fo as to crufh his nofe, or beat out his teeth, by
rufhing fuddenly upon him, is allowable.

The ranks of officers differ from ours : thofe
only who command line-of-battle fhips, and frigates carrying 18-pounders, are properly ftyled
captains. Other frigates are commanded by
lieutenants ; and veffels of 20 guns or under
by enfigns. Common courtefy, however, with
them, as with us, annexes the title of Captain to
all commanders. Agreeably to this claffifica-
tion the pay is regulated, but it is at prefent
found fo grievoufly inadequate, as to caufe great
complaints ; and yet the French are unanimous
in affirming, that all ranks are not only better
paid, but better fed, clothed, and treated, than
under the old government. Befides his pay,
every officer, including the warrant officers and
midfhipmen, is allowed a *traitement*, in lieu of

E the

the table which was formerly kept at the king's
expence. The *traitement* of admirals and captains is very handfome, and fuited to their rank,
as they are enjoined to keep feparate tables:
that of Captain le Franq is 24 livres a day.
No half-pay has yet been fettled upon, or even
promifed to, the French officers. The feamen
are divided into four claffes: the pay of the
higheft clafs is 40 $\frac{1}{2}$ livres a month; of the fecond 36 $\frac{1}{2}$; of the third 33 $\frac{1}{2}$; and of the loweft 30 $\frac{1}{2}$.

Their gradations of command are very fimilar to our own, from the captain to the lieutenants, enfigns, and boatfwain. The office of
pilote, which formerly anfwered to that of mafter with us, is abolifhed. It is particularly enjoined, that the officers be put at five watches,
if the ftate of the fhip will allow of it. The
lieutenant of the watch is ftuck up on a little
pedeftal, which overlooks the helmfman,
whence, except in emergencies, he never ftirs
during his guard, the enfign appointed to
affift him, who is diftinguifhed by wearing a
gorget, being charged to fuperintend the execution of his orders.

§   The

The general uniform of both their navy and
army is a blue coat, with a red waiſtcoat and
breeches: the naval facing is white edged with
red, and that of the ſoldiery red; both ſervices
wear gold epaulettes. The naval button is an
anchor, ſurmounted by the cap of liberty, and
encircled by the words " *La République Fran-*
" *çaiſe.*"

Of the minute regulations eſtabliſhed for
dividing prize money, I cannot ſpeak; but the
general principle on which its diſtribution is
founded appears to me worthy of attention.
Two-thirds of every prize are put into a common ſtock, which is ſhared by the whole navy,
and the remaining third is divided among the
captors. A captain receives but in a propor-
tion of 5 to 1 to a foremaſt-man; a captain of
troops, and a naval lieutenant, as 4 to 1; a naval enſign, ſubaltern of troops, ſurgeon, and
commiſſary, as 3 to 1; midſhipmen, boatſwains,
gunners, &c. as 2 to 1; and quarter-maſters,
and the loweſt rank of officers, as 1 ½ to 1.
The firſt part of this ſyſtem, which relates to
the common ſtock, were valuable, if it could
be impartially carried into execution; but from

E 2 the

the daily fluctuation of the parties concerned, 1
do not fee how it could be reduced to practice
among us, without giving rife to perpetual law-
fuits. Some modification of the latter part
would render its adoption very defirable in a
country where, hitherto, this important part of
the reward of naval toils has been apportioned
with the moft cruel and infulting contempt of
the feelings and neceffities of the lower orders.

Drugs and inftruments of furgery are, I apprehend, very fcarce at prefent in France, as
hand-bills are diftributed over the fleet, enjoin-
ing the officers who may board prizes to be
particularly careful in preferving them for the
ufe of the republic. Thofe belonging to our
furgeons were feized upon this pretence; and,
notwithftanding reprefentations were made to
reclaim them, as private property (which they
were) they were neither reftored, nor an equi-
valent for them offered. Every French 74-
gun fhip is allowed a furgeon and five affiftants.
How many lives might be faved in our fleets,
were our medical eftablifhment equally liberal!
Permit me here to obferve to you, that the fa-
culty owe obligations to the revolution. It is
well

well known that they were heretofore, in
France, treated in many inftances highly unbe-
coming the regard fo juftly due to a profeffion,
whence mankind derive fo many benefits. Surgeons on board (and I am told on fhore) are
now confidered with all the refpeét due to gentlemen, and live in the fociety of the principal
officers.

The French marine corps, which, fimilarly
to ours, was inftituted for the fervice of the
navy, is abolifhed, and troops of the line embarked in their room, who are fubjeéted, by an
exprefs order, which I have read, to all the
general regulations of the crew, and placed
under the abfolute command of the fea-officers.
The detachment on board this fhip belongs
to a regiment in the Weftern Pyrenees : it is
compofed of ftout healthy young men, who, if
not formidable from difcipline and knowledge
of taétics, are full of energy and republican en-
thufiafm. I muft here remark a vulgar error,
which prevails too much among Englifhmen
who have never travelled out of their own
country—that the lower orders of the French
are puny debilitated creatures, inferior to ourfelves in phyfical powers. Could thefe perfons

E 3   be

be prefent at a mufter of the feamen and foldiers of this fhip, they would find their fize and
ftrength the fame as their own, and in hardi-
hood they are certainly ·fuperior to us. I never
before faw people fupport cold fo well ; this is
owing to their having no ftoves on board to
heat themfelves by, a privation which extends
to the officers, not from election but neceffity ;
for Admiral Bligh's ftove was immediately tranfported ·to La Montagne, for Admiral Vilaret,
and one which belonged to the ward-room of
the Alexander, became the prey of Monfieur
de Nieully.

All their men feem to be well fupplied with
clothing. It is furnifhed to them by the government at an eafy price, which has remained
the fame, while on fhore it has been trebled.
Of this they are obliged to keep up a ftated
quantity, and whenever men are turned over
from one fhip to another, a lift of their clothes
is fent with them, and if it falls fhort of the
prefcribed regulation, the men are forbidden to
be received. Each man is fupplied with a ham-
mock and two rugs, but no bed. In cafe men
belonging to fhips are compelled by bad weather, or any other caufe, to remain for the night

on

on fhore, there is a receiving-houfe, to which they can retire, where they are both fed and lodged until they can be fent on board.

The allowance of every perfon in the fleet, without diftinction, is as follows, and like every thing elfe is *decimalized*, or regulated by periods of ten days. On four of them they have half a pound of frefh beef, on two of them half a pound of falt beef, on two of them half a pound of falt pork, and on the remaining two four ounces of falt fifh, with oil and vinegar to eat with it; one pound and a half of foft bread daily—no butter or cheefe: on frefh-meat days, a foup for dinner made of the beef, with a little thickening in it; every evening a foup compofed of four ounces of rice, peafe, or beans, and oil; a wine quart of thin claret daily—fuch is the ration in port. At fea, falt beef and pork are ferved on the frefh-meat days, and, except in exceedingly bad weather, bread is every day baked; when this cannot be done, the fame quantity of bifcuit, of an excellent quality, is iffued. I have feen them grin, when grinding it, at a recollection of its fuperiority over the black unpalatable ftuff, which, they fay, bore the fame name

E 4 under

under the former government. You, who
well know the allowance ferved in our navy,
may, if you pleafe, compare the two inftitutions, and decide which is preferable. I am of
opinion that this is beft calculated to preferve
health, particularly in long voyages and hot
climates; but how far Britifh feamen could be
brought to relifh its adoption, is not fo evident.
Obferve that thefe pounds are *French*, which
exceed our common weight by full two ounces;
and that nominal or purfer's pound, which is
ufed by order on board our fhips, by a great
deal more.

I remember to have formerly treated the
meafure of fending a frigate off Breft, to count
the number of the fleet, or to fee whether it had
failed, more lightly than it deferved. I now
fee that both roads may be infpected, particularly the outer one; and even of the inner one
a fufficient degree of information may be generally gained by a good glafs. The French
boaft of the holding-ground in Breft-Water;
but if I may judge from the frequent dragging
of anchors which happens in moderate weather, it muft be far inferior to that of Spithead.

The

The truth is, they are in general fhamefully carelefs in mooring their fhips: they over-lay each other's anchors, and thereby caufe foul berths, without reflection or ceremony.

Of real feamen they have few left, many thoufands of their beft having been drafted early in the war, and fent to ferve as foldiers on the frontiers. Robefpierre (whofe execution was certainly the triumph of humanity, but not of the allies) by annihilating their foreign commerce, deftroyed the only nurfery which can ever fupply the confumption of a numerous navy. Their fhips are, therefore, filled with landmen, who, previoufly to their being drafted for actual fervice, are fent on board certain veffels fitted on purpofe, where they are taught all the elementary parts of practical feamanfhip. The number of boys on board is likewife very great, and for their inftruction (as alfo for that of fuch men as may be defirous of improvement) a fchoolmafter is allowed to every fhip, whatever be her fize. It is enjoined, that thefe preceptors be capable of teaching the theories of navigation, gunnery, fortification, and the common parts of the mathematics ; and farther,

ther, that they be men of good moral characters, and great fuavity of manners.

They have a naval committee for examining
of midfhipmen and inferior officers, to determine whether they be qualified to take charge
of prizes. Nothing fhort of irremediable neceffity will juftify a commander for entrufting a
prize to the direction of any perfon who has not
undergone this examination,

They water their fhips in the roadfted from
floating tanks, which are brought alongfide,
whence the water is forced by pumps through
hofes into the cafks on board.

Every fhip is furnifhed, at the public expence, with a fuperb fet of charts of every part
of the known world : thofe of our country are
particularly excellent : there is hardly a little
harbour in Britain or Ireland which is not laid
down in them. With us this important charge
is left to the prudence and honefty of a mafter; and how many accidents have befallen our
fhips by a neglect of it, need not be here enu-
merated.

I am affured, that there are in the dock-yard
here three covered docks, under which the
                                    workmen

workmen can carry on their operations in all weathers.

An experiment, of covering by a ftrong wooden cafe the rudders of fhips to the water's edge, which leaves them only juft room to work, is now trying on two or three of their frigates. It is intended to prevent the rudder from being unfhipped, if ftruck by a fea.

The ponderous guns with which they ufed to overload their fhips are difplaced for others of a fize more manageable. No fhip now carries heavier metal than a French 36-pounder. Their firft rates have fixteen ports on the upper and middle deck, and fifteen on the lower, except La Montagne, whofe upper and middle deck are pierced with feventeen ports, and her lower with fixteen; fo that, exclufive of thofe on her quarter-deck and forecaftle (twenty in number) fhe mounts exactly 100 guns. They do not, however, in any of their fhips, turn their quarter-decks to fo much advantage as they might. In this fhip the five aftermoft and moft ufeful ports are blocked up by ftanding cabins, and have no guns provided for them.

When

When the fleet weighs anchor, each ſhip's
ſignal to heave up is made in ſucceſſion. This
method prevents the confuſion which we experience in weighing all together; but, on the other
hand, it precludes that emulation to be firſt,
which a competition cauſes; they are accordingly very tedious in performing this operation.

Official *bulletins* of all public events, which
the convention find it their intereſt to pro-
mulge, are printed on board La Montagne,
from a copy tranſmitted from Paris, and diſtri-
buted, at the expence of the government, to the
officers and ſeamen of every ſhip. This is a
popular meaſure, which wonderfully flatters the
lower orders, who deem themſelves in poſſeſ-
ſion of all the ſecrets of ſtate, and conclude
that politics are no longer a myſtery. I frequently read theſe chronicles, which are always
filled with details of victories over their foreign
enemies, and addreſſes to the convention from
the departments. I was greatly diverted in
reading one of the latter, from the " Popular
" Society " at Breſt, on the occaſion of the
Alexander's colours being preſented to the
convention,

convention, by the Major of Admiral Nieully's
fquadron, who was difpatched exprefsly to
Paris on this important miffion.—" Behold,"
fays the orator, " *Pitt* himfelf virtually brought
" to the bar of the convention, when the Bri-
" tifh banner is proftrated before your auguft
" affembly !" Notwithftanding this flourifh,
and fifty more of the fame fort, I am told that
the inhabitants are ftrongly fufpected of incivifm, and clofely watched.

It has been cuftomary to extol the French
fignals, as fuperior to our own ; but any man
capable of judging, who will compare the two
codes, muft be convinced, that thofe now in
ufe in the Englifh fleet are more fimple in
their principle, more exact in their arrange-
ment, and more eafy in their comprehenfion.
The French were long our mafters in this art,
which lately our naval officers have certainly
carried beyond them. Their fuperior dexte-
rity in making and anfwering them muft not
be confounded with the fignals themfelves. In
this refpect, from being earlier and more clofely
trained, I fear it will be found (though with
many exceptions on our fide) that they furpafs
us.

us. There is on board every French ſhip a
claſs of youths, called *pilotins*, who attend ſolely
to this part of naval duty. They are placed
under the direction of an experienced quarter-
maſter, and hold a rank immediately below that
of midſhipman, into which body they are pro-
moted from time to time, according to their
merit.

Of their deficiency of naval ſtores every day
furniſhes me with freſh proofs. The ſhips by
which we were taken had, after a cruize of a
few weeks, ſcarcely a coil of rope to repair
their running rigging, or a ſtick to ſupply any
loſs which a ſudden guſt of wind might have
occaſioned. But how deſperate muſt the ſtate
of France have been, had the American convoy
been intercepted by Admiral Montagu ! You
know already in part my ſentiments on that
extraordinary failure. Let me now give you
freſh cauſe for amazement; but remember, that
I quote the words of another perſon without
aſperity, and without pretending to aſſign to
what quarter the culpability of that ſhameful
miſcarriage on our ſide attaches : —Admiral
Villaret ſaid a few days ſince, to a Britiſh officer,
                                                    who

who was in Admiral Montagu's squadron:
" *Were you not astonished to see me chase you, on*
" *the 9th of June last, with my crippled fleet?*"
—" *Yes*," was the answer.—" *My only reason for*
" *it was, if possible, to drive you off our coast, as*
" *I momently expected the appearance of the great*
" *American convoy, the capture of which would*
" *have ruined France at that juncture. Why you*
" *did not return to the charge, after running us out*
" *of sight, you best know. Had you kept on your*
" *station two days longer, you must have succeeded,*
" *as, on the 11th of June, the whole of this*
" *convoy, beyond our expectation, entered Brest,*
" *laden with provisions, naval stores, and West*
" *Indian productions.*"

If my cheek reddens on recording this declaration of an enemy, it is with indignation
only.

Hitherto I have not witnessed among the
French, either here or in the prison-ship, a
single trace of divine worship. The *Decadis*
are indeed distinguished by a more than ordinary chanting of republican songs, a display of
the tri-coloured flag on the tops of the churches
in the town, and by a party of officers going on
shore

fhore to the play. Thus, it feems, liberty wants perpetual refufcitation, while the adoration, or even the confeffion, of a Deity, is left to the un-affifted operations of the human mind. From the pompous flimfy reports and orations on this fubject made in the convention; from the *condefcenfion* of Robefpierre, who *decreed* the ex-iftence of a Deity, to the hardy denial of Du-pont, who proclaimed himfelf an atheift; muft I deduce all I know of the prefent ftate of reli-gion in France. It is, however, worthy of re-mark, that a book, intitled " The Republican " Catechifm," which is in univerfal circulation, and exprefsly compofed for the inftruction of the youth of the community, does not once ac-knowledge, or even hint at, the being of a God; and the public inftructor of the prifon-fhip af-fured me, that, although the minds of men be now fomewhat returning to their former biafs, fix months ago an inculcation of this principle, fo far from being prefcribed by the legiflature, would have fubjected the teacher to punifh-ment. God forbid! that, on fuch flender *data* as I profefs, I fhould ftigmatize all Frenchmen with the horrid appellation of atheifts, or even

fuppofe

fuppofe that a belief in revelation is univerfally
fubverted : it were almoft to affirm that it had
never exifted. I have, indeed, in many converfations, had the misfortune to hear innumerable blafphemies uttered, and innumerable
farcafms thrown on all worfhip; but as they
have proceeded from none but weak and ignorant men (to the honour of my friend the
fchoolmafter, he always reprobated them) who
poffibly take this method of recommending
their republican zeal; I fhall be very cautious,
until able to acquire better information, of af-
ferting what are the general fentiments of the
French on this head. Whenever the fubject is
ftarted, the people, among whom I am condemned to live, faften immediately upon fome
of the monftrous abfurdities of the Romifh
church, and the impofitions of the priefthood,
which in truth offer but too fecure a hold for
derifion and contempt. This trick, of attempting to confound the impofitions of knaves, and
the reveries of fools, with the fpirit of Chrif-
tianity, is too ftale and defpicable to deferve
confutation. I will not even quote the noble
and decifive fimile of Hamlet, which feems to

F   have

LETTERS FROM FRANCE

have been conceived on purpofe to expofe it.
Tremble not, therefore, for the faith of your
friend, from fuch puny opponents. He will
not yield his affent to new fyftems, until he
has, at leaft, fcrutinized and weighed their
effects upon thofe who inculcate and practife
them; and if, upon this teft, he finds the pro-
feffors of thefe doctrines to be men of profligate manners and corrupted fentiments, with
the words truth, honour, humanity, and generofity in their mouths, while they are ef-
tranged from their hearts, you will not fuppofe his danger of converfion to be immi-
nent.

And now to terminate this long defultory
epiftle, which I have written by fnatches, when,
and how, and as, I could.—Suffer me, however,
before we part, to fay a word or two of the
political changes which I perceive to be working. My refidence among the French is not
yet fix weeks old; and in this fhort fpace of
time, wonderful has been the alteration of opinion. When we were taken, I was perpetually
ftunned with the exclamations of " *Vive la*
" *Montagne! Vivent les Jacobins!*" But fuddenly,

La

La Montagne is become the theme of execration, and the Jacobin club is cashiered. I
gained a confirmation of these events oddly
enough. I had observed the difuse of these ridiculous cries for some days, and had overheard
a conversation which had raised my suspicions.
To ascertain their justness, I bade one of the
boys call out as before. " Ah!" said he, " that
" is forbidden; *à présent il faut crier, au diable*
" *la Montagne! A bas les Jacobins!*" which he
immediately ran along the deck exclaiming.
The memory of Robespierre they have uni-
formly affected to hold in abhorrence; but if
I may truft to a hint, which was imparted to
me on board the prison ship, very different was
once the tone of Captain Le Franq, and all his
officers. They now load the character of this
extraordinary man, before whom, not six months
since, they proftrated themselves like reptiles,
with all the affaffinations and mifery which have
overfpread France during the last two years.
To him alone, it feems, every crime which stains
the national character is imputable. At prefent I will not venture any opinion; but when
I get on shore, I shall direct my enquiries to

F 2 develope

develope the character of this celebrated demagogue.

The fleet is preparing to fail; and as all the
line-of-battle ships are known either to the
Admiral, his two young gentlemen, or myfelf
I shall be enabled, by obferving which fail, and
which do not, to note down exactly its ftrength,
provided we be not gone before it.   But to-
morrow we are affured we are to be landed.
——Adieu.

LETTER

LETTER V.

La Normandie, prifon-fhip,
Breft-Water, 5th Feb. 1795.

COULD what I write reach you in due courfe, my prefent place of date might furprize you, after the affurances which my laft held out of going forthwith to Quimper. Admiral Bligh has been meanly and cruelly treated: their violated promifes to me are of lefs confequence.

On the day after I laft wrote to you, matters refpecting our departure feemed to be drawing to a favourable conclufion. An officer from Admiral Villaret waited on Admiral Bligh, to beg his acceptance of a loan of one thoufand livres in paper (offering at the fame time as many more as might be wifhed) and to affure him, that we were to be landed on the follow ing day. The livres were accepted; and, as we now deemed our departure certain, we put ourfelves, at day-light next morning, in a ftate of preparation for our removal. Removed, in-

F 3   deed,

deed, we were, not to Quimper, but to this horrid receptacle, where we have been closely immured ever since, suffering every mental punishment which low-minded rancour and brutal ignorance could inflict; and every physical hardship which this rigorous winter, and occasional deficiencies of food, could produce. I have not seen a fire during the whole month of January; and on Christmas-day I was one of *fifteen* English officers, with the Admiral at our head, whose dinner consisted of *eight* very small mutton-chops, and a plate of potatoes. This last circumstance, exciting both hunger and indignation (as we knew that a *traitement* was paid for us by the government, and as we had lately from our encreased number lived by ourselves) we determined not to bear it without remonstrance, especially as for several succeeding days our treatment had been little better; and I was delegated to inform the officers of the ship, that if they should not use us hereafter more liberally, we would write a complaint against them to Admiral Villaret. This produced a good effect; and henceforth we were more amply supplied. In justice to Monsieur Villaret, I must

observe

obferve to you, that his character is eminent for
honour and juftice ; and in fpite of appearances
againft him at firft, on our not being fent to
Quimper, we now know, that had his ability
been equal to his difpofition, Admiral Bligh
would not be here. Of Le Franq I cannot
fpeak in fimilar terms. He exhibited a mean
exultation at our difappointment, not altogether
unaccompanied with infult; and his whole behaviour, for fome time before we left him, had
entirely altered our firft impreffion of him.

Our detention has, however, been productive
of a very defirable event to the Admiral. In
confequence of a late decree of the convention,
directing that all women and children who had
been captured fhall be liberated, and permitted
to return home, he was enabled to fend away
his fon, under the aufpices of Lady Anne Fitzroy,
who had been a prifoner for many months at
Quimper.

The fleet failed from the outer road on
the 30th of December, confifting of the following fhips, under the command of Vice-
Admiral Villaret, who was affifted by the
Admirals Bouvet, Vanftable, Nieully, and Renaudin:

F 4

naudin, and controlled by feveral reprefentatives.

	Guns.			Guns.
La Montagne, -	- 120	Le Jean Bart,	-	- 74
Le Majeftueux -	- 110	La Convention,		- 74
Le Terrible, -	- 110	La Revolution,		- 74
Le Revolutionnaire, -	110	Le Scipion,	-	- 74
Le Neuf Thermidor *,	84	Le Neftor,	-	- 74
L'Indomptable, -	- 84	Le Mutius Scævola, -		74
Le Tigre, -	- 74	Les Droits de l'Homme		74
Le Montagnard,	- 74	Le 31 de Mai, -		- 74
Le Tourville,	- 74	Le Neptune,	-	- 74
Le Pelletier, -	- 74	L'Eole,	-	- 74
L'Acquilon, -	- 74	L'Entreprenant,		- 74
Le Temeraire, -	- 74	Le Trajan,	-	- 74
Le Zelè, -	- 74	Le Patriote,	-	- 74
L'Audacieux, -	- 74	Le Gafparin, -		- 74
Le Marat, -	- 74	Le Superbe,	-	- 74
Le Tirannicide, -	- 74	Le Redoutable,		- 74
Le Jemappe, -	- 74	Le Fougueux,	-	- 74

And the Alexander, of 74 guns, with at leaft a dozen
frigates, and feveral corvettes.

Le Republicain, of 110 guns, was intended
to conftitute a part of the fleet; but on the
night of the 24th of December fhe broke from

* Formerly Le Jacobin, the fhip fuppofed to be funk
on the firft of June.

her

her anchors, was driven on a rock, and bulged, in a manner which does very little credit to French feamanfhip. Here fhe lay until the 9th of January, when her remains were burned, her main-maft and mizen maft being then ftanding, and her main-tcp fail yard acrofs.

When the fleet failed, the wind was nearly at E. and it continued to blow here between the points of N. E. and E. S. E. until the evening of Sunday the 25th of January, when it fhifted to South, and next day blew frefh at S. W. On Thurfday the 29th of January it returned to S. E. and continued in the Eaftern quarter until the evening of the 31ft, when it backed to S. W.

On the 12th of January Le Redoutable fingly came back into port; on the 28th feven fail more of two-deckers returned, having parted three days before in a fog from the body of the fleet, which, to the number of twenty fail, arrived on the fecond and third of this month, and two others have got into l'Orient: *no lefs than the following five having either foundered, or been purpofely run on fhore, to prevent their finking.*

Le

		Guns.
Le Scipion,	-	- 74
Le Superbe,	-	- 74
Le Neuf Thermidor,	-	84
Le Temeraire,	-	- 74
Le Neptune,	-	- 74

The condition even of thofe which have efcaped, is deplorable : among others Le Ma-
jeftueux had four pumps going when fhe entered the port. Two days ago I held a long
converfation with the Captain of Le Jean Bart,
who execrated the planners of this deftructive
expedition to their navy. He affured me, that
it had been remonftrated againft in the ftrongeft
terms by the naval officers, and its pernicious
confequences foretold; but the orders from
Paris were pofitive. The fleet cruized in three
divifions, the eafternmoft of which kept but
juft outfide of Scilly and Ufhant; and the
wefternmoft was once driven as far as 18° W.
in the latitude of 45°; the central divifion oc-
cupied the intermediate fpace. I learned thefe
particulars from fome mafters of Englifh mer-
chantmen who were taken, and have been fent
to this prifon. A more effectual plan to interrupt

terrupt our commerce could not have been
devifed. Of its practicability, had I not lived to
fee it executed, I fhould at leaft have doubted;
but this is an age of political phænomena on
the water, as well as the land. Between fifty
and fixty prizes were captured by this fleet,
among which was a tranfport bound from
Ireland to Briftol, having on board 120 foldiers of a new-raifed regiment, who are now
confined here, and do fo little credit, by their
appearance, to Britifh troops, that I have more
than once blufhed, when they have been pointed
at by the French; and I have been afked with a
fneer, " Are thefe the men who are to march
" to Paris?" In the lift of prizes were alfo fix
or feven of the homeward-bound Oporto fleet,
all of which they funk, with their cargoes;
deeming, I prefume, that honeft beverage (to
ufe the words of one of their authors) " a heavy
" ftupifying liquor, fit to be drunk by Englifh-
" men only."

Cut off as I am from all communication with
Englifh politics, I fhall not prefume to guefs at
the caufes which have retained our fleet in harbour.

7

bour. But fome of thofe which have not retained it, I fhall venture to ftate. It was not
the weather, for that was uninterruptedly fine
until the 25th of January. It was not the
wind, for that during the fame period was always eafterly, here at leaft, and our diftance
from Plymouth is barely 45 leagues. It was
not a want of information, for (to my knowledge) exclufive of other channels, two Englifh
gentlemen, who efcaped from this place in a
boat at leaft as early as the 8th of January,
muft have arrived in England by the 12th or
13th. The rigid caution obferved by the
French, in not hazarding engagements at fea,
is notorious. In the prefent inftance it has
been exchanged for a hardy audacity. They
now boaft that they have challenged us to the
lifts, which we have not dared to enter againft
them; but, during the time of their fleet being
out, I have feen them tremble at the probability
of fuch an event. Had the month of January
been as tempeftuous as it commonly is in this
climate, our affiftance would hardly have been
required to deftroy their leaky and crazy fhips,

in

in want of naval ſtores and able ſeamen. One
hard gale of wind at S. S. W. would have coſt
them at leaſt a dozen ſail of the line.

What then ſhall we ſay? "There is," my
friend, "a tide in the affairs" of nations, as
well as of men: the page of hiſtory every
where records it. Hannibal, after the battle of
Cannæ, inſtead of marching to Rome, turned
aſide to Capua; — from that moment the Car-
thaginian fortune ebbed, never to flow again.
The ſeries of rapid conqueſts, which diſtin-
guiſhed the brilliant campaign of 1776, was
finiſhed, not by taking Philadelphia, diſperſing
the Congreſs, and breaking up the new government, but by occupying winter cantonments in
Jerſey, where our victorious army was beaten
in detail;—and America was loſt. The allies,
after the ſurrender of Valenciennes, divided
their forces; — and ſince that fatal ſeparation
how has their career of conqueſt been turned
into retreat, marked only by overthrow, conſternation and deſpair!

On the 31ſt of December, the Admiral was
again reduced to my ſociety, and that of his
youngſters, all the other officers of the Alexander

ander being fent on fhore to the Château,
where, according to accounts which I have received from them, by fome letters privately
conveyed to me, they are treated in a manner
fhocking to humanity.—But I muft be contented with telling you my own ftory.

On their departure we who were left were
again taken into the mefs of the officers of
the fhip. The military part of this affembly
are a fet of worthlefs wretches; but two of
thofe who fill civil pofts are men of honourable
characters, ever ready to pity our fituation,
and to give us every reafonable degree of intelligence of the ftate of the country, and what
is going on; to which I add the advantage of
reading daily fome of the Paris news-papers,
which are brought on board.

Through thefe channels I draw not only
abundant matter for reflection, but frequently
obtain diverfion. " Moderation, and down
" with the Terrorifts !" refound, I believe,
from one end to the other of the republic. It
is in all refpects our intereft to wifh that fuch
fentiments may be more than nominal. It is
certain that a general difmiffion of the creatures
of

of Robefpierre is taking place. The indifcriminate advancement of unqualified candidates
to offices of truft and dignity, which to court
popular applaufe univerfally prevailed until
lately, furnifhes to thofe, who are not over-
friendly to a democratic caufe, an inexhauftible
fund of merriment and ridicule. Among others
who have juft experienced the inftability of honours is Tribout, who commanded the troops
at Breft. This man, from beating a drum, and
officiating as a regimental barber, under the
old government, had been advanced by the revolution to the dignity of a drum-major,
whence, by an eafy gradation, he at once rofe
to the rank of a general officer, for intrepidity
difplayed in a battle on the frontiers. His elevation, however, only expofed him to derifion
in the diftrict wherein he was delegated to
command. Like the unfortunate cat, who at
the requeft of her mafter was metamorphofed
by Jupiter into a young woman, and who ftill
retained her feline appetites, fome unlucky
trait, it feems, was for ever occurring in this
poor man's behaviour, to remind the fpectators
of his earlier profeffions. When he was on
the

the parade he had all the flourishes of the drum-
major, and at table all the busy curiosity and
oily language of the *frizeur*. After exciting
universal contempt against himself and his em-
ployers, during the period of his command
here, he has been suddenly stripped of his full-
blown honours, and condemned to vegetate
hereafter on a small pension, which has been
assigned to him ; with permission, however, to
retain the title of *General* Tribout.

The 21st of January was the anniversary
of the execution of Louis XVI. an event which
will be annually commemorated by very different ceremonies and emotions from what dif-
tinguished this day, when the political phrenzy
that now agitates Frenchmen shall be evaporated. A play analagous to the occasion
was performed at the theatre, *gratis* ; the towers
and forts on shore, and all the ships in the harbour, displayed their colours; and lastly, to
prove their civism, the *keepers* of this dungeon
put on their best clothes, and provided the best
dinner I have seen since I have been taken.
I ate of it, but not without a sigh for the cause
which gave birth to this savage exultation over
the

the manes of a mild and generous, though
irrefolute, monarch.   And even here I feel
pleafure in faying, all fenfations of pity are not
extinguifhed, all diftinctions which fhould re-
gulate the adminiftration of juftice are not obliterated.   This very day a Frenchman whifpered in my ear, " His death (the king's) in
" fpite of the veil which the convention threw
" over the real fentiments of the people, ftruck
" the hearts of the majority of Frenchmen with
" amazement and horror."   Of the memory
of the queen he fpoke lefs affectionately.   He
recounted to me fome of the extravagant tales,
which have been fo induftrioufly propagated
againft her; but in defiance of them, what un-
prejudiced mind can hefitate to pronounce,
that the cruel and ignominious rigour of her
confinement; the brutal and unmanly fpirit that
dictated the charges upon which fhe was tried;
and the mockery of all juftice with which fhe
was profecuted; joined to the violent death
inflicted upon this unhappy princefs (againft
whom report has been fo loud, and proof fo
feeble) have fixed upon the annals of the revolution a ftain, which will be indelible, while

G   fentiments

fentiments of tendernefs and generofity towards women, and principles of equity towards the accufed, are cherifhed in the human
breaft ?

The news of the entire conqueft of Holland
has caufed great rejoicings. But when the
wildnefs of joy and congratulation had fub-
fided, what think you was the firft reflection
which I heard on the fubject?—A calculation
of the advantages which will accrue to their
marine. By this acquifition, they hope to be
enabled to difpute the empire of the fea with
England. It is publickly reported, that a ne-
gociation for peace with Pruffia is proceeding,
and will be fpeedily completed; but to this I
only oppofe my filent unbelief.

We often hear of Charette; but the accounts
are fo extravagant and contradictory, that I
know not what to think. About two months
ago I was perfuaded, from all I read in the news-
papers, and from what I was every day told,
that he had either furrendered, and fworn fealty
to the republic, or was about to do fo; but as
the moft furious republicans among my prefent
affociates have lately been filent about him, and

answer

anfwer with reluctance to my queſtions on the
fubject, I can only guefs, from their referve,
that all is not agreeable to their wiſhes, and confequently that he is ſtill the rallying point of
royaliſm.

I have fometimes my doubts whether it be
not their intention to continue us where we are
altogether, and that the promiſe of being fent
to Quimper is as deluſive as every other part
of their conduct; but theſe are only the fug-
geſtions of fpleen, on recollecting the frequency
of our difappointments; for an order is abfolutely received on board, to fend us hence to a
ſmall armed brig, which is to take fome coaſters
under her convoy to Quimper, as foon as the
wind ſhifts to the N. W. In her, it feems,
and not according to the firſt intention of fending us by land, are we to be conveyed to our
place of deſtination. — There ! — but hang
gloomy anticipations ! the thought alone of
being on ſhore, and able to warm myfelf by
exercife, muſt give it a decided preference to
a prifon - ſhip, in which, during this bitter
feafon, we have been cooped up, and frozen
both in foul and body. You would have

G 2   laughed

laughed to fee the contrivances we have had
recourfe to, to keep up a little warmth, and re-
ftore circulation to our benumbed extremities.
The Admiral twice wrote to the reprefentatives, for permiffion to walk on fhore with
the officers of the fhip; but of his firft letter
no notice was taken; and to his fecond only a
verbal anfwer, that " his requeft could not be
" granted," was returned.———Adieu.

LETTER

LETTER VI.

MY DEAR FRIEND, Quimper, Bretagne,
18th Feb. 1795.

Lucky! lucky dog! you will exclaim, when you read the word Quimper at the head of this letter; and are farther told, that I am comfortably lodged, and feated at an Englifh table. This welcome intelligence will, I think, foon reach you through a channel by which I fhall venture to fend you a packet.

We arrived here yefterday: Admiral Bligh brought with him a letter from an Englifh lady, who accompanied Lady Anne Fitzroy, to Mademoifelle Brimaudiere, a native and inhabitant of the town; and, on prefenting it, was obligingly told by her, that fhe had already received notice to prepare for him, from a gentleman at l Orient, whofe fon-in-law, the captain of the America, was a prifoner in England; and that if he pleafed to accept of fuch accommodations as her houfe, which was a hired one, afforded, they were at his fervice. This cour-

teous

teous offer, you may be fure, was immediately
clofed with, and we took poffeffion of our new
apartments. Here we were alfo welcomed by
two of our countrymen, whom we found to be
inmates of our houfe—Lieutenant Robinfon,
late of the Thames frigate, and Mr. Burley,
of the fame fhip. With thefe gentlemen we
have formed a mefs. The good lady of the
houfe condefcends to market for us; our fervants, affifted by the maid of the houfe, officiate
as cooks; and we live already fo much more
comfortably than I ever expected to do during
my captivity, that I cannot defcribe to you the
joyful fenfations I have experienced on this
change.

We quitted the prifon-fhip on the 14th inftant, to our unfpeakable fatisfaction. From
our military acquaintances there we parted without an adieu, from our civil ones not without
fentiments of efteem. For the laft nine days
before our departure we had feparated from
their mefs, and lived entirely by ourfelves, owing to the following circumftance :—On fome
Englifh prifoners being brought on board, one
of the officers of the fhip, who is a Provençal,
                                                and

and fpeaks fo indiftinctly, that his own countrymen cannot, without difficulty, underftand him,
defired one of our young midfhipmen to inter-
pret for him, which requeft he would readily
have complied with, as he had often done before, had he comprehended it; but not poffeffing the gift of underftanding inarticulate founds,
he turned round to his companion, and faid,
" Monfieur ——— afks me fome queftion, but
" as ufual I don't know what it was." The
other not hearing himfelf called upon, and not
fuppofing the matter to be very important,
fmiled, and both of them, in all the gaiety and
thoughtleffnefs of fourteen, walked away. For
this enormous offence they were immediately
fent for into the cabin, and, without being fuffered to urge a fyllable in explanation, were
told, that they were not any longer to confider
themfelves as entitled to eat at the table of the
officers. The young gentlemen communicated
this to me, and I loft no time in informing the
Admiral of it; who finding, on examination,
that they had not committed an intentional in-
civility, defired me to explain the bufinefs, and
to affure Monfieur——— that the apparent

flight

flight had proceeded from mifapprehenfion.
This I attempted to do, and in return for it was
honoured with feveral fcandalous appellations,
as an inftigator and abettor of the offenders, although it happened that I had not been prefent
when the crime was committed. Our two
friends in the civil department alfo attempted
to interfere in their favour, but were filenced by
authority, the infult being deemed of a public
nature, and ftriking at the dignity of the republic. Admiral Bligh now declared, that if the
young gentlemen were to be thus driven from
the mefs, he and I fhould look upon ourfelves
as included in the expulfion. This they would
willingly have prevented, and wifhed to draw
a line of diftinction; but the Admiral's manly
refolution cut fhort debate, and, on their refufing to yield the point, he and I directly quitted
them with contempt; and with two fpoons belonging to our fervants, and a pocket-knife
each, which conftituted our whole ftock of uten-
fils, we fet up our mefs forthwith, demanding
our rations, but refufing to receive any more
traitement. Now was to be feen, for the firft
time, in a civilized enemy's country, a Britifh
Admiral,

Admiral, whofe feat was a trunk, and whofe
table was a trunk, eating a falt herring laid on
a fcrap of paper, from want of a plate; or fup-
ping at the fame board, with a candle ftuck in
an ink-horn, on a fecond herring; or dipping his
fpoon in a tub that held our foup, which was
part of that made for the fhip's company, fometimes of beef, and fometimes of horfe-beans
and oil. Breakfaft, however, by having a little
tea and brown fugar of our own, with the addition of fome falt butter, which we had procured from the fhore for our fervants, was a
repaft of real luxury. This miferable fare, and
want of common neceffaries, lafted but two days,
when we got leave to employ the cook to market for us, and drefs our provifions. It brought
me, however, perfectly acquainted with the
extent of the French allowance, and likewife
with the prices of different commodities on
fhore, which we found enormoufly high, and
every day rifing. To confole us, however, the
value of gold, in exchange for *affignats*, more
than kept pace in its increafe.—Here I take
my leave of the good fhip La Normandie, and
her worthy inmates, in full truft that, in the
courfe

courfe of our future correfpondence, neither her name, nor theirs, will ever again pollute my paper!

My obfervations fince I left Breft could not be numerous; but, as I feel an intereft in them, they fhall not be fuppreffed.

The little veffel which conveyed us hither was extremely inconvenient, and ill-fitted for the purpofe; but her commander, Monfieur Confeil, and his officers, treated us with great civility and regard. She had been a Jerfey privateer, and retains her Englifh name, the Betfy. About noon, on the day before yefter-day, we anchored juft within the mouth of the river that leads to Quimper, within twenty yards of the fhore. After fo long a refidence on fhip-board, amidft men of coarfe and fero-cious manners, I could not withdraw my eyes from the fcene before me. It was a clear frofty day, but the deep fnow of the winter had been melted by intervening thaws, and the fields bore that frefh and verdant hue, which is fo re-animating to the human heart. The river was of a moderate breadth, and on each fide ftood a parifh-church, furrounded by a few

fcattering

scattering houses. Notwithstanding the keen-
ness of the weather, the peasantry were dancing
in circles in the open air. The small space
which I could see bore no trace of distress or
devastation; and so transported was I with the
appearance of all around me, heightened by a
recollection of the past, that I was almost ready,
with the shipwrecked philosopher of antiquity,
to cry out to my companions, " Courage, my
" friends! from these marks I know we are
" thrown among civilized beings !"

Our commander, who was of a pleasant un-
suspicious temper, begged that the Admiral
would defer going up to Quimper until the
next morning; and offered, if we pleased, to
accompany us on shore after dinner for a walk.
This was a welcome invitation, and eagerly
embraced. About two o'clock we landed with
our conductor, and set out for a large handsome
looking house, the *château* of the Marquis de
Kersalaun, about a mile off, which we had seen
in the morning, in running along-shore, before
we entered the river. We passed through thick
woods, and when we reached the *château* found
there an engineer, who is stationed on the coast,

in

in the fervice of the republic, and is a friend of
the Marquis. This gentleman is permitted to
refide here, and alfo two of the Marquis's old
female fervants. He received us very politely,
and led us up large ftone ftaircafes, through
various apartments lined with old tapeftry, and
half illumined " by rich windows, which almoft
" exclude the light." He fhewed us alfo a fmall
chapel within the houfe, which, though commonly kept fhut up, bears marks of the fury of
the times. The *château* is long and low, with
a turret, which refembles a pigeon-houfe, on its
centre, and has a fine old avenue leading up to
it from the fea-fide. Before we left the houfe,
the gentleman prefented to us fome excellent
cyder, and lamented, with evident figns of mortification, that he poffeffed not a drop of either
wine or brandy. From the houfe he took us
into two large walled gardens, forming oblong
fquares. In the difpofition of thefe, and the
other grounds furrounding the houfe, no mark
of tafte appears, but they exhibit the hand of
wealth and labour. In the centre of the largeft
garden ftands a circular bafon or fountain of
confiderable fize, " which once," faid our civil
                                                    and

and fenfible conductor, " was thought an em-
" bellifhment to the *château*. Here," continued
he, " ran the leaden pipes which fupplied it,
" and here were fixed the plates of iron which
" fecured it; but, as you fee, all the former
" are dug up, and caft into bullets, and all the
" latter have been torn off in wantonnefs. Mark
" too the breaches in that wall, through which
" the cattle and pigs enter; and how the efpaliers
" are either broken, or rooted up. No means
" to prevent thefe depredations are left in my
" power. The *château* was lately converted
" into a temporary prifon, to contain a party
" of Englifhmen, who, under the guard of a
" detachment of foldiers, were fent to cut down
" the Marquis's woods, for the ufe of the re-
" public. I have lefs caufe of complaint
" againft the Englifh than againft their guards,
" who were to the laft degree infolent and de-
" ftructive. Twice did they fet fire to the
" houfe by their carelefsnefs"—(we had feen the
marks on the floors and tapeftry)—" I com-
" plained and remonftrated againft them, in
" vain, to our municipality: I obtained no're-
" drefs. But this evil was temporary. The fatal
                                            " change

" change which has taken place in our manners,
" and the wide-extended fpirit of rapine, which
" it has introduced, has infected our peafantry.
" The farmers and tenants of the Marquis,
" who formerly preffed forward to ferve him
" (for he was a kind and generous landlord) are
" now eager to promote the devaftation, and
" to fhare in his fpoils. This and this," (pointing to different marks of fury and ravage)
" have they committed."—As we went home-
ward he made us obferve, that all the trees of
the avenue were marked, for the ufe of the republic; " and," added he, " are all to be cut
" down foon, with the reft of the wood on the
" eftate, in order to be fent to Breft, the whole
" being in a ftate of requifition." I faw fome
large groupes of ftately firs, many of which were
felled and fquared on the fpot. I put fome
queftions to him about the Marquis and his
fortune. " He is," faid he, " between eighty-
" one and eighty-two years old, and is now at
" Paris, where he is obliged to refide, and, in
" return for ftripping him of his eftate, he has
" been *promifed* a penfion. Perhaps, as matters
" are certainly foftening among us, he may be
                                    " enabled

" enabled to make better terms. It is not pre-
" tended that he has committed any crime ; but
" he fuffers for thofe of his two fons, who have
" emigrated; and, at the age of fourfcore years,
" he was thought too dangerous a perfon to be
" permitted to dwell on his hereditary eftate,
" where he offered to remain tranquil, and fub-
" miffive to the ruling powers. He was for-
" merly *Doyen* of the States of Bretagne. In a
" letter, which he lately wrote to a friend, he
" ftates himfelf to be in good health, and to have
" borne the exceffive cold of the winter very
" well; but complains that wood was 400
" livres a cord, and meat three livres a pound.
" The value of his eftate was between fixty and
" feventy thoufand livres *per annum* ; but of
" this to the amount of not more than twelve
" thoufand lies contiguous to the houfe. The
" timber, however, on this latter part was fo
" valuable, as to be reckoned at twice the
" worth of the land."—It appeared to me, indeed, to be very thickly wooded.

We bade adieu to our obliging informer, and
returned towards our 'fhip, by a different way
from that which we had come. On this road I
                                          ob erved

obferved three or four ftone croffes, broken
and thrown down. When we reached the land-
ing-place, the peafants were again dancing, with
fome foldiers, failors, and fifhermen. We went
clofe to look at them, and, except from one
lady, who told us, in broken French, fhe did
not like the Englifh, met with neither rudenefs
or infult. The figure of their dance was very
fimple, confifting only of defcribing a circle,
through various parts of which, with joined
hands, they threaded from time to time; and
notwithftanding their wooden fhoes, I thought
they executed it with more fpirit and lefs awk-
wardnefs than our clowns generally perform.
None of the women were handfome, but they
had all healthy cheerful countenances, and were
coarfely but cleanly dreffed; their long white
caps, which form a fort of hood behind, giving
to the younger ones a very fober and matron-
like appearance. A publick-houfe, which the
dancers of both fexes frequently vifited, was
clofe by, where cyder and a fmall acid red
wine were retailed. Thefe people converfed
entirely in the Breton language, the found of
which, had I not forcibly felt from other circumftances

cumſtances where I was, would have made me
ſwear that I was in Wales. I found, upon
trial, that not one in ten of the peaſants could
ſpeak French, or even underſtood it when
ſpoken to them. I aſked if the gaiety which
I ſaw was continual, or only occaſional; and
was told, that this was the week of the *carnival*,
a period of feſtivity, which the Bretons of all
ranks, notwithſtanding the auſterity of the
times, have never failed to celebrate in revelry
and diſſipation.

I went into ſeveral houſes. They form a
medium between the neatneſs of an Engliſh,
and the filthineſs of an Iriſh, cottage; they are
dark and gloomy like the latter, but the walls
are ſtrongly built of ſtone, the roofs well
thatched, and none of them are without a
chimney. There was a moderate quantity of
neceſſary houſehold utenſils in all, and a good
fire burning, over which, in moſt of them, hung
large pots boiling. Here was no indication of
want or diſtreſs. " Deſtruction to the châteaux,
peace to the cottages," is an aphoriſm, which
has been often repeated in the convention, to
inſtigate the poor to plunder the rich.

H   The

The church-door being open, I walked in, and found it converted into a barrack for the foldiers belonging to a fmall fort which ftands at a little diftance. There was a large fire burning in it, and it was filled by the bedding and other effects of the men; but I obferved that the altar was entire. A ferjeant, feeing me regard it with attention, whifpered me, that it owed its prefervation to him: a piece of intelligence of which I could not doubt the truth, when he carried me into a little veftry, which he unlocked with a key that he took from his pocket. There he fhowed me the images of our Saviour and the Virgin, which were here depofited uninjured. I commended the zeal of this honeft halberdier, and we parted good friends, it being time to return on board.

Next morning after breakfaft we were conveyed hither, in one of the fhip's boats. The diftance is about three leagues; and a cold eafterly wind blowing ftrongly againft us, made the paffage tedious and difagreeable. The river winds very much, and gradually narrows, until it becomes contracted at Quimper to a frefh-water brook, deep enough, however, to permit

veffels,

veffels, which do not draw more than eleven feet,
to reach the town at high water. Its banks are
highly picturefque, very woody, and rather wild
and bold than fertile. They are befides adorned
by many gentlemen's houfes, on a fmaller fcale
than the Marquis de Kerfalaun's *château*, but
built in the fame tafte, and furrounded by plan-
tations of fir-trees. Like the *château* too, they
all bear marks of the unhappy ftate of the country, the windows being broken, the garden-walls
and fences deftroyed, and an air of defolation
fpread around them.

About one o'clock we reached Quimper, and
were taken to the houfe of the commiffary of
prifoners, whofe reception of us did not forebode
the pleafing confequences which followed; for
this man of power, when acquainted with our
names and ranks, neither did us the honour to
return our falute of the hat, or to afk us to
fit down. However, after having given a receipt for us to the captain of the veffel, he con-
defcended to conduct us in perfon to the houfe
of Mademoifelle B—— (to whom he is related)
whofe polite and obliging reception of us, foon
caufed us to forget the republican manners of
Citoyen Precini.

We have found here abundance of our countrymen, this town being the principal *depôt* of
prifoners of war in the Weftern departments.
In this unfortunate lift are Captain Kittoe, of
l'Efpion floop of war, and his two lieutenants;
Colonel Caldwell, who is a native of Ireland,
and in the Portugueze fervice; with many other
officers and gentlemen, and feveral hundred
Britifh feamen.

LETTER

LETTER VII.

Quimper, 2d March, 1795.

ALTHOUGH placed in a part of France
very remote from the capital, and unfrequented by travellers, I find in all I hear and fee
abundant matter of wonder and reflection; and
as I advance in my enquiries, the fcene continues to open upon me. To witnefs the me-
ridian blaze of the revolutionary government, I
am arrived fix months too late; its difaftrous
luftre is eclipfed. When I teftify emotions of
aftonifhment, I am always cut fhort by the ex-
clamation of, "Ah! if you had been here in the
" reign of Robefpierre, or even during the firft
" three months after his death!"

I am not upon any parole, either written or
verbal, but I am *cautionné*, that is, the lady of
the houfe is bound for my appearance at all
times, in the fum of 3000 livres. Upon this
confideration I have leave to go into all parts
of the town, and have ventured to deviate, in

H 3   every

every direction, into the furrounding country, to the diftance of two or three miles, without having hitherto met with interruption.

Nothing could happen more fortunately than our coming here at the beginning of the car-nival-week, during which parties meet every night at each other's houfes. The evening of our arrival the meeting was held at Made-moifelle Brimaudiere's, and was attended by all her friends and acquaintances, who, as fhe is a woman well born and connected, are of the better order, though, as I found in the fequel, of very oppofite political opinions. Formerly thefe affemblies were clofed by fumptuous fup-pers; but in the prefent poverty of the times, they meet only to play at *paffe-dix*. Into this circle I was introduced, and found the greater part of it compofed of well-dreffed people of both fexes, who furrounded a large table, on which the dice were rolling, and the fpirit of betting as keen as it could have been at any former period; handfuls of *affignats* fhifting their owners every moment; and even children, of not more than feven or eight years old, were encouraged to ftand by, and receive leffons in this inftruc-
tive

tive feminary:—" *Ma mere! dix fols pour !*—*Ma*
" *tante! quinze fols contre !*" refounded from infant mouths on every fide. Among the women
were feveral whom I thought very agreeable in
perfon, particularly Mademoifelle Kérvélligan,
and la Marquife de Ploeuc. The latter is extremely elegant in her manners, but beams
" with faded fplendor." I could not bear to
hear the boorifh and difgufting title of " *Ci-*
" *toyenne*" applied to a fafhionable woman ; and
therefore, whenever I addreffed myfelf to the
marchionefs, I called her " *Madame la Mar-*
" *quife,*" and the reft of the company *Made-*
moifelle, or *Monfieur.* Indeed to this I had acquired a fort of right, by being myfelf honoured
with the appellation of " *Monfieur le Major,*"
when I was invited to play, which I at once
accepted, and formed one of the circle. Thefe
good old-fafhioned courtefies alfo fell occa-
fionally from the reft of the company; but I
obferved that they were fpoken in a low voice,
and not without trepidation : they are, however,
I am affured, faft returning into vogue.

At a play-table the common centre of union
muft be the ftake, and to that I found here, as

H 4 elfewhere,

elsewhere, all cares anxioufly directed; but,
during fome fhort ceffations of the game, I remarked that the company divided into knots,
which feemed jealous of each other. The operation of a more powerful paffion being fuf-
pended, their political prejudices were now re-
vived. I was among royalifts, federalifts, and
fierce republicans one and indivifible. The
fathers, mothers, brothers, and fifters of emigrants, for whofe defertion they had been punifhed, collected with *bons citoyens*, and *enragés*.
Of thefe laft, from not mixing in their groupe,
I can fay nothing, except that the drefs of fome
of them was affectedly mean, and their converfation marked by a boifterous and rude familiarity, which I knew before were leading cha-
racteriftics of their party. If I find myfelf compelled by neceffity to cultivate an acquaintance
with any of this faction, while I remain at
Quimper, I hope I fhall not be conftrained to
extend to them an obfervation, which I was
forced to pafs upon their brethren on fhip-
board—that I never knew one man, profeffing
to be a fierce and flaming republican, who poffeffed either the manners which fhould diftin-
guifh

guiſh a gentleman (ſetting aſide the forms of
courteſy) or that common ſhare of probity,
which is required to keep the links of ſociety
together.

In the little knot of royaliſts to which, you
may ſuppoſe, I attached myſelf, I was not worſe
received for being an Engliſhman. Indeed they
ſpoke quite undiſguiſedly before me, but it was
in whiſpers. A young lady, on ſeeing me gaze
with attention upon one of the republican
phalanx, who (like all his colleagues) had worn
his hat during the evening, aſked me, which I
liked beſt, the tri-coloured cockade I was ſur-
veying, or the "*cocarde blanche?*" "The cockade
" of honour, to be ſure," I anſwered.—" Softly,
" ſoftly, for God's ſake!" ſaid ſhe, " or we ſhall
" be overheard and undone."

One of the company, Monſieur Kérvélligan,
is a member of the convention, and appeared
to me, both on this occaſion and ſince, to be a
manly dignified character. I converſed a little
with him on indifferent ſubjects, as he only
played occaſionally. He is reputed to poſſeſs a
penetrating mind; and it is certain that he
very early diſcovered the views of Robeſpierre,
and

and defcribed them faithfully to his friends here. Monfieur Kérvélligan was profcribed, with many other deputies, on the 31ft of May, when the Briffotine party was overthrown, and compelled to flee before that of the Mountain. With fome of his colleagues, he effected his efcape into Normandy, and thence into the wildeft part of this neighbourhood, where he took refuge among the peafants, by whom he was known and beloved. Thefe poor people were well aware, that by betraying him they might make their fortunes; but they were too fimple and honeft to violate the duty of hofpitality. He frequently ventured to come into town in difguife, and has often heard himfelf proclaimed a traitor, and a reward offered to whoever would bring him in, alive or dead, to the municipality. Soon after the execution of Robefpierre, he emerged from his retreat, and by a late decree of the convention, is recalled, with others, to his feat in their body; and intends to fet out to Paris very foon, to refume his delegation. Monfieur Kérvélligan voted againft the murder of his fovereign; and has told his friends here, that in going, on the day of the queftion being put to the vote, to the

hall

hall of the convention, he and many other
members were feveral times ftopped, and furrounded by bodies of the loweft clafs of the
people, who clapped piftols to their heads,
threatened them, and fwore they would facrifice
them on their return, if they did not vote for
the death of their fovereign.

During the carnival-week there was a fecond
party, fimilar to the firft, at our houfe: and,
under the aufpices of our good hoftefs, I went
alfo to two others, the laft of which, on *Sunday*
evening, was at Monfieur Kérvélligan's, where
the fame entertainment was provided, and pur-
fued with the fame avidity. Mademoifelle Kérvélligan I have already mentioned as a handfome young woman; and her mother, Madame
Kérvélligan, is alfo very agreeable.

At one of thefe routs I faw a fpecimen of genuine democratic manners, which all who aim
to become great men in the ftate affect to imitate. The commiffary of prifoners, a man al-
lied to nobility, liberally educated, and once an
Abbé, bolted into the room where the company
were affembled, humming the *Carmagnole*, with
his hat on, which was adorned with a red, a
white,

white, and a blue feather, and his hands ftuck
in his breeches, *not pockets*. In this attitude
he ftood all the evening, and thrufting himfelf
among the ladies, had the impudence to enter
into familiar converfation with the Marchionefs
de Ploeuc, and other women of rank and delicacy, with all the airs which confcious fuperiority of power can inftil into a reptile. This
brutal manner of mingling in fociety, and ad-
dreffing women, has become, fince the revolution, the *ton* of republican coxcombs, and during
the reign of Robefpierre fet decorum and the re-
ftraints of civilized life at defiance. It is now on
the decline, except with thofe who ftill court the
applaufe of the dregs of that faction. A courtier
of Verfailles at his toilet, furrounded by paints,
patches, and perfumery, was, in the eye of reafon,
a ridiculous and contemptible animal; but the
moft effeminate effenced *marquis*, that ever con-
fulted a looking glafs, was furely preferable to
this indecent blockhead.

In frequenting thefe little circles, I fee many
victims of the tyranny of the government, and
hear fuch anecdotes of it related, as make me
fhudder. The marchionefs has been ftripped
of

of two eftates, and the beft houfe in this town,
which is converted into a prifon. Two ladies,
who refide in our houfe, are but juft liberated
from a clofe confinement, under which, with
many more of their fex, they languifhed for
fourteen months. During their imprifonment
in return for the fequeftration of their property,
they were allowed *twenty fols* a day, out of which
they were compelled to pay two for *houfe-rent.*
Monfieur Brimaudiere, brother of the lady of
this houfe, was *capitaine des gens d'armes* of this
diftrict, a poft of truft and power. When the
party of Briffot fell, he was feized, fent to Paris,
and imprifoned for fifteen months in the *Concier-
gerie.* During the whole of his confinement he
was kept in the fame room, and faw, during that
period, 167 perfons go out of it to the guillotine,
every day expecting himfelf to be added to the
number. His fate was clofe at hand when Robefpierre was overturned, and foon after the
death of the tyrant he was liberated, and fent
back hither, to refume his former fituation, which
he now fills. He defcribes almoft the whole of
this affembly of victims to have been fo confcious
of their innocence, and fo reconciled to their
lot,

lot, from the daily exits of their friends, that
nothing but refignation, indifference, or levity,
prevailed throughout the prifon, death having
ceafed, from its familiarity, to terrify. It was
cuftomary to warn, on the preceding evening,
thofe prifoners who were to be put on their
trial the next day; and by a regulation made
among themfelves, the party to be tried gave a
fupper on that night to the whole room; and, if
he was fpared for the prefent, and remanded
back, he was in return treated with a dinner at
their joint expence. " Our dinner entertain-
" ments," faid my informer, " were few in-
" deed; but Oh! the fuppers without end which
" we partook of!"

All my days, however, have not been paffed
in going to routs, and liftening to details of
mifery. I have paid a vifit to two more members of the convention, and have been *at
church*. On the afternoon of the 19th inftant,
the reprefentatives Guefno and Guermeur arrived here in great ftate, in a coach which had
once belonged to their king, drawn by eight
horfes, and efcorted by forty huffars. " *Voila
" l'egalité!*" cried aloud fome (I was told) who

faw

faw them enter in this pomp. " And," faid
my informer, " as if confcious of their power,
" and the importance of their miffion, they
" neither bowed to the crowd which was af-
" fembled to gaze at them, nor fpread any lure
" to engage popular attention, like their brethren
" who have heretofore been among us." They
are both natives of Bretagne, and of good,
though not of noble, families. In conjunction
with feveral more deputies, furnifhed with great
powers, they have been delegated by the convention to treat with the inhabitants of La
Vendee. Among other avowed objects of their
coming hither, is an enquiry into the complaints
which have been at different times made by the
prifoners of war. Accordingly, two days after,
Admiral Bligh, attended by Captain Kittoe and
myfelf, went to the tavern (which once was the
town-palace of the *bifbop* of the diocefe) wherein
they lodged. We faw them both, and the Admiral, through Captain Kittoe and me as his
interpreters, made fome reprefentations to them,
which, if not quite fatisfactorily anfwered, were
at leaft candidly liftened to by Monfieur Guermeur, who was extremely civil; but his colleague
Guefno

Guefno was lefs friendly, and more elevated, keeping his feat, with his hat on, while we remained in the room, and frequently interrupting our ftatements. He is faid to avow publickly a hatred of our nation, which in this fhort conference could not be reftrained. On the following day I was deputed by the Admiral to wait upon them again, with a letter from him, entreating them to give orders that the other cfficers of the Alexander (who are ftill clofely locked up in the *château* of Breft, fuffering mifery and impofition) might be liberated, and permitted to join us here. Upon reaching their hotel, I found a crowd of fuitors attending at the foot of the ftair-cafe; but the landlady, on feeing me, affured me I fhould not wait for an audience, as an order had been given by Guermeur to admit at once all Englifh officers who might wifh to fee him. I profited immediately by this flattering diftinction, and marched through two rows of impatient Frenchmen, who were expecting what I had obtained. I found him alone, and was as politely received as on the preceding day. He read my difpatches with deliberation, and in anfwer defired

me

me to prefent his compliments to the Admiral,
and to affure him, that he would write to his
colleagues at Breft, and beg them to comply
with the requeft.

Liften now to a relation, which will in fome
degree evince to you the infamous height to
which impofition, on the ignorance of the
people, is practifed in this country —On the
23d of this month an exprefs arrived, in the
middle of the night, from the other reprefentatives on miffion in this department to thofe
here, which caufed great fpeculation, affording
to one part of the inhabitants of the place as
much joy and exultation, as to the other it was
productive of grief and difmay:—" *Peace con-*
" *cluded with Charette.*"—An event, at once
fo momentous and defirable, could not pafs
without celebration. A drummer was fent in
the morning into the town, who proclaimed at
the corner of every ftreet the important intelligence; and announced, that on the fame evening a ball, in honour of it, would be given by
the reprefentatives of the people, to which all
good republicans were invited to repair. This
was a bitter trial to the poor royalifts, particu-

I   larly

larly to thofe who had been lately liberated from imprifonment. Many of them, rather than go to fuch a commemoration, chofe to fubmit to the imputation of incivifm, and to provoke afrefh the arm of power; while others, more compliant, went with aching hearts, to wear the mafk of joy on an event, which, if true, quafhed their final hope. They all, however, confoled themfelves in believing that the information was unfounded. "How," faid they, " can we credit any thing which our enemies " tell us? How many victories have not we been " commanded to celebrate, which were gained " only in the fertile inventions of thofe who " fabricated them, and iffued the orders! Did " they not affure us, that the Englifh fleet was " defeated, and almoft utterly deftroyed, in the " engagement of the firft of June? Did not " ——, and ——, and ——, who were juft ar- " rived from Breft, aver with folemnity and " oaths, that they had feen, and actually been " on board, *three Englifh fhips of the line*, in " the port of Breft, which were taken in that " action? &c. &c."

On thefe fpecimens of modern Gallic ef-

I   frontery

frontery I leave you to your own reflections; and shall only observe, that in a very few days the intelligence about Charette was contradicted, when the royalists, as far as they dared, returned the laugh upon their opponents.

Be this as it may, the ball was well, or at least fully, attended, by generals, colonels, captains, serjeants, corporals, privates, and drummers, with their wives and children; to whom may be added all the butchers, barbers, bakers, tallow-chandlers, servant-maids, and fishwomen in and about Quimper, " whose dress, man-" ners, and vociferation, joined to the offensive " smell which proceeded from their persons, " drove me," said the lady from whom I borrow this account, " out of the room in about " half an hour." The maid of our house (who is not of an ignoble stock, although reduced to service) said, she did not deign to dance, as none but *sans-culotte* partners offered themselves. Water was the only refreshment which was served up at this civic feast, and all the fiddlers of the town were put in a state of requisition to play at it. My curiosity was strong;

but

but it was impoffible for an Englifhman to be
prefent on fuch an occafion.

I fhall now defcribe a fcene to you, which
filled me with very different emotions from
this recital.—On leaving the reprefentative,
after prefenting to him the Admiral's letter, as
I was going out of the door, I heard the found
of an organ, proceeding from the cathedral,
which was very near the houfe: I went in, and
found mafs celebrating in the prefence of a
congregation confifting chiefly of poor people
from the country, with a few of the higher
ranks, many more of whom, I was affured,
would have been there, could they have believed themfelves fecure from reproach; but
the return of religious worfhip was yet too
young for them to incur the rifk—they were all
kneeling at their devotions, with great appearance of fervency, while a fine grey-headed re-
fpectably looking prieft, habited in his ponti-
ficals, officiated at the altar. I walked the
whole length of the church, through rows
of people on their knees, which formerly
might have been deemed difrefpect in a he-
retic;

retic ; but I now met with nothing but courtefy and regard, all feeming confcious that the
bafis of their perfuafion and mine was the
fame, however we might differ in external forms
of adoration. Here I had leifure to contemplate the fcene of defolation which this venerable temple prefented. At leaft half the
windows of fine old painted glafs, " richly
" dight," were broken ; all the monuments
torn down; and the bones of the dead expofed
to view, and commingled with the ruins of their
tombs, the names and armorial devices being
utterly defaced, and the coffins taken away and
converted into bullets. When the fervice was
finifhed, I went within the railing which in-
clofes the altar, to look at a large picture, reprefenting the Afcenfion, the figures of which
are pierced through in more than twenty places,
by fabres and bayonets. An old man, who was
kneeling near the rails, obferving my attention
fixed on the painting, told me, that in the va-
cant fide-compartments once ftood two other
pictures taken from holy writ; " But," faid
he, " they were fo cut and hacked, that *we*
" were under a neceffity of taking them away."

I 3   A gen-

A gentleman, who had joined me in the church, informed me, that the altar and confeſſionals which I ſaw had been brought hither from another church; for that thoſe belonging to this had been either burnt, or broken into a thouſand pieces: nay, that the figures, with which the altar had been adorned, were carefully ſeparated from it, and triumphantly guillotined in the middle of the great ſquare of the town.

Cold and republican muſt have been the eye which could ſurvey ſuch ſcenes of barbarous devaſtation unmoved, and the heart which could liſten to ſuch deſcriptions of ſacrilegious delirium without a ſigh!

> " —— Oh! but man! proud man!
> " Dreſs'd in a little brief authority;
> " ——— like an angry ape,
> " Plays ſuch fantaſtic tricks before high heaven,
> " As makes the angels weep."   SHAKESPEARE.

Upon enquiring, I learned that the church had been open for public worſhip about three weeks, in conſequence of a proclamation iſſued at l'Orient, on the 13th of January, by the repreſentatives Gueſno and Guermeur, in which
liberty

liberty of worſhip is granted to all men in their own way, on " proper terms," but not as a national worſhip; the republic diſavowing a national religion, although tolerating and permitting the free exerciſe of all, provided the prieſts who officiate have taken the oaths of allegiance to the ſtate. To this laſt ſtipulation the thinneſs of the weekly congregations is in part attributable, the rigid catholics holding in deteſtation the prieſts who have taken the oaths.——Adieu.

I 4   LETTER

LETTER VIII.

Quimper, 4th of April 1795.

I SHOULD not amuſe you with a diſquiſition on the etymology of the name of Quimper, or a reſearch into the date of its foundation, were I capable of furniſhing ſuch an entertainment ; but I will tell you all I know of its preſent ſtate, and of the country contiguous to it.

It is unqueſtionably a town of conſiderable antiquity, and when it formed a part of the poſſeſſions of the dukes of Bretagne (ere thoſe were annexed to the crown of France, by the marriage of Charles VIII. with Anne of Brittany) ſometimes ſided, in the wars between the Engliſh and the French, with one party, and ſometimes with the other. A maſſy ſtone wall ſurrounding the old town, the cathedral, and ſome other buildings, are believed to be the works of our countrymen.

The town ſtands in a bottom, encompaſſed by high hills, and the largeſt part of it is built on a neck of land formed by the confluence of

two

two rivers. I have often thought it like Plymouth; but it is not fo large, although even
now extremely populous. Its ftreets are narrow,
winding, and dirty; and their former names
have been changed into others of a revolutionary
found, fuch as the ftreet of Voltaire, the ftreet
of Mably, the fquare of Liberty, &c. &c. The
greateft part of the houfes are very ancient and
mean; but a few are large and ftately, with
walls whofe thicknefs feems intended for endlefs
duration. On entering them, I was furprized
to fee the unfinifhed ftate of moft of the apartments, which are uncieled, the bare beams and
crofs-pieces prefenting themfelves to view. I
fhall be within the bounds of truth when I
affert, that of 1500 houfes, which are perhaps
in the town, not fifty have each a cieled room,
and not ten, or even five, have the whole
apartments of the ground and firft floor cieled.
The bottoms of the rooms are as unfightly as
the tops, from the gaping chafms of the planks
which compofe them; and the dirty ftate in
which the floors and furniture are kept, is
difgufting. Neverthelefs in fome refpects the
interior of thefe houfes deferves regard. The
vaft

vaft mirrors which adorn their beft apartments, and the beautiful plate glafs of the windows, far exceed what are feen in Englifh houfes, except thofe of the firft fafhion. The French engravings I prefer to all others, and a few very good ones are ftill left here, though defaced, by having their dedications to princes, *maréchaux de France*, and other great men, very clumfily erafed. Of plate too it is faid they formerly difplayed fumptuous fide-boards; but thefe have difappeared, having been either buried or committed to the crucible. Indeed it was become neceffary to adopt one or other of thefe meafures; for foon after the 10th of Auguft 1792, the democratic luft of deftruction rofe to fuch a height, as to order all family diftinctions derived from anceftry, and all heraldic emblems whatever, to be erafed, not only from the outfides of the houfes, but from every article of furniture. Even the armorial bearings engraved on the moft trifling toys, a fnuff-box, a ring, or a feal, were obliterated; and the poft-office took care to detain all letters, of which the feals were impreffed with thofe fhocking emblems of ariftocracy.

I now

I now eat with fpoons whence the family marks are carefully expunged, the obfervation of which led to my enquiries.

A man who has feen only this fkirting of France would demonftrate the higheft degree of prefumption, were he to pretend to draw a parallel between it and England; but, to confine myfelf to what I have feen here, I may venture to affirm, that civilization, luxury, a general diffufion of the comforts of life, or by whatever other name you pleafe to call it, is more advanced in Cornwall and Wales than it was in this province, even before the revolution.

Formerly there were two public walks on the banks of the river; but the ftately elms which formed one of them have been lately cut down, to the great diffatisfaction of the inhabitants, in order to be fent to Breft for keels of fhips.

The cathedral is a large edifice, of majeftic appearance, but ftrikingly irregular in its exterior. Over its principal door is written " *Le* " *peuple Français reconnait l'Etre Suprème.*" All the other churches and monafteries, which are numerous, have been converted (as the property of the ftate) into hofpitals, ftables, magazines,

zines, or manufactories of falt-petre. The
church applied to this laft ufe is well adapted to
the purpofe. I went with an Englifh gentleman to fee it, and no objection was made by the
people whom we found there at work to our in-
fpecting every part of their procefs, which is
very fimple. — Againft one of the fide walls are
piled large heaps of wood-afhes, and near them
two rows of cafks with perforated bottoms,
which are filled with the afhes thoroughly wet-
ted. The water, after paffing through the afhes,
is received into tubs, and conftitutes a vegetable alkaline lixivium. The oppofite fide of the
church is filled with the ruins of old houfes, and
heaps of earth dug out of ftables, flaughter-
houfes, and cemeteries, which laft are full of
the wrecks of humanity. Thefe, after being
macerated and mixed with the liquor drained
through the wood afhes, are evaporated over a
flow fire, until exhaufted of the fuperfluous wa-
tery particles; after which the remaining part
is put into large fhallow coolers, on the fides of
which the falt-petre fhoots into cryftals.

The workmen employed here are only twelve
in number, and the quantity of falt-petre made

is

is about fifty pounds a day, which, according to their account, cofts only four livres and a half a pound; but this muft not be depended upon, for they did not know the quantity of wood confumed. The wages of thefe people are inconceivably low, only 50 fols a day, and a ration of bread. Until lately they were paid only 35 fols, the addition having been made in confequence of the increafing dearnefs of the neceffaries of life: even now 50 fols will fcarcely buy a pound of the'worft veal brought to market. They complained of its infufficiency, and told us, that manufacturers in England were paid as much for two hours work; " but, neverthelefs, " it is for the republic." Either from this conjecture of the liberality of our country, or from fome other caufe, they treated us with particular refpect, and anfwered all our queftions with the moft ready civility: not an interefted civility, for they neither received, nor gave us room to fuppofe that they expected, any gratuity.

I quitted the place with ftrange fenfations. The procefs which I had witneffed was whimfically fhocking. When I faw amidft the earth the bones toffed about, " mine ached at the re-
" membrance."

" membrance." This earth, faid I to myfelf,
once, perhaps, belonged to men whom thefe
houfes fheltered, and againft whofe defcendants
in La Vendée it may, when fabricated into the
breath of deftruction, volly forth, in the fhape of
bullets, the coffins which once enclofed their
forefathers. There is certainly no difcovery
which entitles to higher admiration the inven-
tive genius of man, than that of artillery, in all
its wonderful combinations; but, at the fame
time, it muft be confeffed, that no ftronger
proof of our miferable degeneracy and infa-
tuation can be produced, than our application
of it.

The bifhop's town-houfe I have mentioned.
At a diftance of lefs than a mile down the river
ftands what was once his country refidence; but
it is now the property of a naval officer, who
bought it at a fale of national domains. I walked out to it the other day, and found it neither
very large, nor very magnificent. It commands
a good profpect of the river, and is pleafantly
fituated at the head of a large garden, filled by
ftone fteps and ftrait walks. I found a gardener at work in it, who fhewed me a fuperb
orangery,

orangery, where, in large wooden cafes, ftand
the fineft orange and lemon-trees which I ever
faw growing out of their native climes, and
bearing ripe fruit in the month of March.   I
afked the gardener about the laft bifhop, who
was a conftitutional one, and was told, that he
was guillotined about a year ago, at Breft, for
being a federalift.   I had heard fo before.—
" Was not he," faid I, " dragged away fud-
" denly, and denied the confolation of taking
" leave of his family, who were in the houfe ?"
—" I believe," anfwered the gardener, " he was;
" but thofe things were fo common fome time
" fince, that no body attended to them.   I
" mind my work, and afk no queftions."—I
gave him an *affignat* of fmall value, which he
expected, and went away.

But a building which would have excited my
curiofity more than the palaces of bifhops and
the houfes of nobility, I arrived here too late to
fee—a Temple of Reafon, built for the exercife
of the new religion of France.—It ftood on the
fummit of a lofty hill, clofe to the town, and
confifted only of a few pofts, from which rafters
met at the top in a point to fupport the roof,

the

the fides being open.   Within it was adorned
by feftoons of oak-leaves, and was backed by a
tree of liberty. It was the favourite rendezvous
of the party of Robefpierre, under whofe auf-
picious reign it was erected.   Here they fwore
eternal enmity to kings, and extirpation to ariftocrates; and here their dances and fports were
held, and the laws were read.   In July laft (not
above ten days before the fatal *neuf Thermidor*)
all the unmarried young women, and even all
the children of the town, down to feven years
old, were compelled to march in proceffion up
the hill, preceded by the mayor and a band of
mufic, and to take an oath never to marry any but
true republicans and *fans-culottes.* About three
months ago this edifice was either blown down,
or its foundation fecretly undermined in the
night; and only a few broken pofts and a little
thatch now proclaim, " *Ilium fuit.*"

If the ftories which are told of the extrava-
gancies which this place gave birth to did not
come from thofe who witneffed them (both
French and Englifh) their poffibility might be
doubted. I fhall trouble you with only one of
them.—A young republican of this town, on
being

being ordered as a foldier to the frontiers, took
a young woman of the place, and fwore her here
to be true to him; but even this teft of the
reality of her intention not being fufficient to
quiet his jealous fcruples, he abfolutely wrote a
letter to the convention, which was laid before
them, ftating his fituation, and intreating that
the girl might be put in a ftate of *requifition*,
in her maiden capacity, until his return; left, in
his abfence, fhe might be expofed to the allure-
ments and feductions of ariftocrates, who went
about feeking to injure good republicans and
fans-culottes like him. Can it be believed that
a national congrefs fhould afford a ferious hearing to fuch nonfenfe? Yet fo it was; and fhe
was actually commanded to remain fingle until
the young man fhould return.—Not a very
gallant compliment to the lady's conftancy of
temper, you will fay! To do juftice to the
French, I muft however obferve, that all
ranks and parties of them now deride the remembrance of thefe degrading follies.

There are two coffee-houfes in the town,
which are numeroufly reforted to by both the
Fnglifh and the French, notwithftanding an in-

K   fcription

scription placed over the door of one of them, forbidding any but good patriots to enter. The sign of this coffee-houfe gave rife lately to a refined piece of affectation :—it was a lion devouring a human body, and fo exquifitely fufceptible are the feelings of the prefent reigning party become, that they ordered the man of the houfe to blot out the body, " *it fo reminded them* " *of the days of Robefpierre.*" Accordingly the lion only now is feen. Here I go daily to read the Paris newfpapers, and meet not with any interruption. For this privilege it is expected that fomething be fpent: a difh of excellent coffee cofts 15 fols, and a glafs of *liqueur* from 20 to 40 fols. Perfons of all ranks and profeffions, officers, foldiers, and their wives, and the people of the town, mingle here promifcuoufly.

The market-place is fpacious and convenient. In the centre of it ftands, on a fquare pedeftal, a ftatue of Liberty, with infcriptions on each fide, fome parts of which have been recently white-wafhed, to obliterate them. Among thefe I could decypher the word "*Mon-* " *tagne,*" and a few others of analogous fignification,

cation, which a change of opinion has suddenly
expunged from the vocabulary of French pa-
triotism. — The market-day is still Saturday,
when patroles of soldiers are sent on all the
roads which lead to the town, to prevent fore-
stalling, by compelling the country people to
bring all their commodities into the market-
place. Besides large heaps of wooden-shoes,
the market generally affords some poultry and
game, but not much butchers meat, except lean
veal, of which I have never seen a want. Fish
would be plentiful, were the boats permitted to
go to sea; but, from a fear lest they should give
information to the English, the fishermen are
either interdicted, or subjected to so many diffi-
culties, by being compelled to give security and
take soldiers in their boats, that most of them
have given up their employment. Of bread I
have not since I have been here seen any deficiency; but I have been informed it was once,
in the depth of last winter, so scarce, as to occasion a proclamation to be issued, that whoever
sold it to a prisoner of war should be punished.
We have always been able to procure it for
assignats. It is for the most part very brown and

K 2   coarse,

coarse, but some whiter and finer is made, and
publicly exposed to sale, in spite of the law, or-
dering only *pain d'egalité* to be used, which every
body laughs at, and nobody thinks proper to
enforce. The worst quality of all this bread is
a grittiness, being full of small sandy particles,
arising from two causes—the softness of the grind-
stones—and the corn not being sufficiently wash-
ed, after the oxen have trodden it out, which is
practised here instead of thrashing. This may
serve to evince, in how small a degree calcu-
lous complaints are generated, by swallowing in
our food similar materials to those of which
stones and gravel in the human body are com-
posed. The Bretons are remarkably healthy,
and, I have been assured, are in general free
from those diseases. Neither has any symptom
of them been found among the English prisoners.

The prices of all articles in the markets and
shops are increasing every day rapidly, owing to
the depreciation of *assignats*. France is nominally dear, but to a man who possesses gold it is
at present, perhaps, the cheapest country in the
world. Meat is three livres a pound, and tolerable

lerable wine eight livres a bottle; but then a
guinea will openly fetch 300 livres, and a *louis
d'or* 350 ; the difference arifes from the ignorance of the peafantry in regard to the former,
and their confequent diflike to exchange them.

There is yet a little coafting trade carried on
here. It was once more confiderable, but they
never had any foreign commerce. The fhops
are numerous, but not overftocked with commodities, and the fhopkeepers always recom-
mend their goods, not only to us, but to their
countrymen, by faying they are " Englifh,"
which is too true : they are the fpoils of our
merchants. I have been well informed, that
previoufly to the war a prejudice in favour of
our productions ran fo high here, and over all
this part of France, that hardly an article of
drefs and furniture of French manufacture could
be fold. You cannot conceive with what avidity thofe prifoners who are artificers are fought
out and employed. You will laugh to be told,
that one of the reprefentatives, either Guefno
or Guermeur, fent for an Englifh fhoemaker to
make him a pair of boots, and even prolonged
his ftay for a day, rather than depart without

K 3   them.

them. Perhaps a better fpeculation than to fend
here a fmall cargo of out popular manufactures,
in a veffel drawing not more than eleven feet,
when peace fhall be reftored, and liberty of exchange unfhackled, could not be projected.
France will then open her *mines of gold and filver.*
In other words, immenfe quantities of fpecie and
other valuables, which are at this day buried,
will be dug up and brought again into circulation. Some part of thefe concealments will undoubtedly be loft to their owners; who, after
having entombed them, have either been chafed
from their native foil to return to it no more,
or elfe have paid the debt of nature without
communicating their fecret. Ages hence their
children will turn them up from the bofom of
the earth; and, on feeing the effigy of the moft
unfortunate of kings, will recal to remembrance
the moft calamitous period of the hiftory of their
country.

Nothing furprized me more, on my arrival
here, than to fee beggars in every part of the
town. The French officers at Breft had affured
me, that there were no longer any in the republic; the government undertaking to make a
provifion

provifion for thofe, who might have no oftenfi-
ble means of fubfifting. In confequence of this
intelligence, I had dreffed up a fine fpeculation,
in favour at leaft of one change effected by the
revolution.—If, faid I, the noble and opulent
are ftripped and have fallen, yet the oppreffed
and miferable part of the community have
emerged from that gulph of wretchednefs, into
which, under the ancient government, the moft
numerous clafs of inhabitants were plunged.
The country, which has not in it any citizen fo
deftitute as to want a fufficiency of food and raiment, cannot be fo unhappy as we in England
are fond of reprefenting it.—What then was
my aftonifhment, on entering Quimper, to find
in every ftreet, and in its environs, wretches
of both fexes, who, with a livid afpect, and in
a faltering voice, folicited of paffengers a morfel
of bread to appeafe their hunger, or that of a
ftarving hufband, wife, or child ! It was in
vain to anfwer me, that thefe perfons, by application to the municipality, might be relieved ;—
fo may all our poor, by applying to the work-
houfe or parifh-officer; but who, neverthelefs,
will venture to affirm, that we have among us

no

no victims of hunger?—As I advance in my actual obfervations I gain a knowledge of facts, which lay open the real ftate of the country, and better enable me to appreciate the condition of the people, and the evils derived from equality incorrectly underftood.

The inhabitants of this town formerly con-fifted, befides the working people, only of petty fhopkeepers, and of many of the neighbouring gentry, who, though not nominally rich, were able, in this cheap quarter, to keep town-houfes, in which, during the winter, they refided in great plenty and hofpitality. Thefe patricians are faid to have held the *bourgeois* at an immea-furable diftance, but to have been very chari-tably difpofed towards the wants of the poor. The tafte for gaming, which I have fpoken of, is not new. It always flourifhed here; and formerly, during the week of the carnival, and fome other feafons of feftivity, it was not un-common to find adventurers here, who had made a journey from Paris to get a pluck at the *Nobleffe Brétonne.*

For two miles around the town I know the country pretty well, having always been fond

of

of walking and making excurfions. In thefe little rambles I keep, however, in the moft unfrequented tracks, and always meet with civility from the peafantry, though by the foldiery I have been twice compelled abruptly to return. The parts I have traverfed are diverfified by hill and dale, and very like the wilds of Devonfhire, with a ftream dafhing through every bottom. There are innumerable copfes, but large trees, except firs, are hardly ever feen. The foil is almoft univerfally light and fandy, and abounds in lime-ftone. Every cottage has an orchard, but the cyder is not reckoned equal to that of Normandy. I often infpect the labours of the hufbandmen, and wifh I could talk to them. Except fome fine meadows near the town, through which two beautiful ftreams flow, the ground is chiefly employed to raife corn. The corn fields are very neatly divided into lands, and their implements of hufbandry, particularly their wheeled ploughs, are much fuperior to what I had expected to find. Neverthelefs, either from the lightnefs of the foil, or want of fkill on the part of the cultivators, the crops of wheat are very moderate, not above

five

five or fix for one.—They raife a few parfnips,
and feed their horfes with them to great advantage; but I have not feen one field of turnips,
cabbages, or carrots, as a winter ftock for cattle,
and very little clover. I have not yet converfed with any man, who has the leaft knowledge of what a fucceffion of crops means: to
fallow feems to be the only affiftance which they
give to worn-out grounds. They teftify only
ignorance and amazement, when an Englifhman
explains to them the attention beftowed upon
this important part of farming, and a cultiva-
tion of artificial graffes among us. Potatoes
are yet planted only in gardens and fmall
patches; but the culture of them every day extends, having more than once been recom-
mended by authority. They frequently call it
la racine Anglaife, and many of the young people
relifh the potatoe; but their fathers and mothers, to whom until lately it was a novelty,
prefer the moft ordinary vegetable to it. It is
a very common practice to irrigate not only
meadows, but higher lands, which demonftrates
an intelligent fpirit; the little troughs, which
fteal along through almoft every field the ftreams
which

which the bounty of nature has supplied to the country, are well contrived, and answer, as I have observed, effectually. Upon the whole, what I have been able to see and hear of the management of grounds here, notwithstanding the great deficiency I have pointed out, exalts it above the humble opinion which I at first sight formed of it. You know my fondness of agricultural pursuits, and the impediments which have constantly arisen to prevent my indulgence of it.

The cattle are very small and mean, worse, I think, than any breed I ever noticed in the wildest part of North Wales, and certainly inferior to the moor breed of Devonshire and Cornwall. I speak only of countries which I know. Even in the meadows, though better, they are unaccountably small, considering the pasture. The sheep are proportionably diminutive. Admiral Bligh and I had one day the curiosity to put in the scales a hind quarter of lamb, which was purchased in the market for our table, and it weighed, the kidney and a bit of liver included, exactly—*thirteen ounces and a half.*—At Brest we had remarked the

§   smallness

fmallnefs of the meat brought on board, feveral
of the quarters of mutton not weighing more
than three or four pounds each. The horfes
are low and hardy, but, by continual impor-
tations from other parts of France, are very
fuperior to the cattle and fheep. The women
here ride aftride.

The houfes of the peafantry are like thofe
I defcribed on my landing. I fhould oftener
enter them were it not for dogs, which are
chained clofe to the doors, by one of which I
was feized by the thigh, and bitten through a
thick pair of trowfers. Certainly the diftreffes
of the times are greatly felt by all ranks of
people in France; but in the cottages I have
never feen want. One of the chief articles of
the meals of the peafants is a fort of pancake,
called *crape* (I fpell like an Englifhman) made
chiefly of buckwheat flour, and eaten with
milk. Thefe people are, indeed, a feparate
race from the body of the French, and have a
language and cuftoms of their own, to which
they are tenacioufly attached. I much lament
that I cannot fpeak Welch, although fo many
of my happier days have been paffed in Wales.

As

As to French, it is of no more use to me among these natives, at the distance of half a mile from the town, than if I were at Ispahan or Delhi. Almost all the gentry can speak this language. The Bretons and Welsh preserve another resemblance: the latter do not love *cwrw* (ale) better than the former do brandy. The evening of a market-day here presents as drunken a scene as I ever beheld in England; but these good folks do not appear to be so quarrelsome in their cups as ours generally are.

The diocese of Quimper stands in a district called Cornwall. The truly old British words *Pen*, and *Caer*, are affixed to the names of innumerable places in the circumjacent country; and mark the origin of this people, were we to seek no other proofs.

The town is surrounded by the *châteaux* of the gentry. Very few of the right owners live in them, and many of them are going fast to decay. Every where I see the dove-cotes demolished, which were the earliest victims of the first revolution; and I cannot lament their overthrow. The game-law now established
gives

gives liberty to every one to kill what game he may find upon his own ground, or that which he rents; and if any perfon, without leave, fhoot on his neighbour's ground, he pays for each offence a fine of ten livres. How fu-perior is this fimple regulation, conceived in a fpirit of equity, to a perplexed and odious code of penal ftatutes for the prefervation of hares and partridges! Let me bring you acquainted with two other laws, which owe their birth to the revolution.—One of them is juft paffed, and exempts from the punifhment of death, even after delivery, women who are tried for any crime when pregnant. " Can a woman fo fitu-
" ated," afks the framer of the decree, " be-
" come a mother in that tranquil ftate of mind,
" which is fo neceffary to enfure the phyfical
" good of her offspring? Befides, could we
" forget humanity, does not the republic act
" impolitically in probably preventing the birth
" of a new citizen; (for women in this condi-
" tion almoft ever mifcarry) or in condemning
" the mother to bring forth a half-formed being,
" which is ufually diftorted in mind and body,
" incapable of ferving the ftate, and of propa-
" gating

" gating its fpecies?"—I am fure I hear you join me in unqualified applaufe of the principle of this humane and confiderate inftitution. — The other interdicts a duel, in all cafes whatever, under the penalty of death to the furvivor or furvivors.—The late king of Pruffia faid, that to determine whether fingle combat, in certain cafes, ought, or ought not, to be aboliſhed, required a congrefs of all the monarchs in Europe. Had he lived to witnefs the ſhocking grofsnefs of fpeech and manners, which prevail among modern Frenchmen, for want of this or fome other curb of a private nature, I think his uncertainty would have vaniſhed, without troubling the crowned heads to affemble.— At leaft mine has.

The French often boaft of the unexplored fubterranean treafures of their country; and fome among them are fanguine enough to believe that they ſhall rival England in her collieries. There are near Quimper two veins of what is called *charbon de terre* worked; but I have been affured by an Engliſh furgeon, that on analyfis he found it to be *not coal.* I picked up a piece, one day, at the mouth of a pit,

carried

carried it home, and put it into the fire, where
it became red-hot, without confuming. To
what ufe it is applied by thofe who extract it,
I know not. It is, however, certain, that they
have feveral times been induftrious in trying to
find out miners among the Englifh prifoners;
and in a few inftances have fucceeded in fe-
ducing our men to go and work at fome mines
(of what I do not know) which are faid to lie
near Breft.

The inhabitants of the town, or troops of
the municipality as they are called, are obliged
to do the ordinary duties here, when the regular foldiers are abfent. In certain cafes, however, they are allowed to perform this fervice
by proxy. The prefent price of a fubftitute is
ten livres a day, which is judged to be more
than the worth of a day's labour, though it
will not purchafe more than a pound and a
half of bread, a pound of veal, and a bottle of
indifferent wine.

I have not yet faid any thing to you of the
French regular troops whom I have feen fince
I have been landed. There is not at prefent
any complete regiment here, but there are de-
tachments

tachments of infantry from feveral. Every day
I fee the different guards parade, march off,
and relieve; and twice I have feen a detachment exercife, and perform their evolutions,
which, though few and fimple, were very awkwardly executed. Certainly a ftranger, who
fhould neglect to calculate the force of other
caufes, would ftart, on being told, that before
thefe raw levies (to ufe Mr. Gibbon's words,
as nearly as I can recollect them, on an occafion
not very diffimilar) the difciplined legions of
Germany, the fons of chivalry of Caftille, the
gallant nobles of their own country, and even
the hardy freemen of Britain, have been compelled to flee. In vain would he look for thofe
ufual indications of excellence, and prog-
noftics of fuccefs, filence, attention, and the
exact performance of movements in a great
body, which we find in an individual.—In their
room he would fee battalions, compofed indeed
of ftout and healthy young men, but clumfily
and confufedly drawn up, with uneven ranks
and broken files, whofe bold looks, flovenly
attire, and unreftrained carriage, would feem
to proclaim equal defiance of their enemies and

L their

their leaders. Talk to them, and they will try to make you believe, that they wiſh to decide all battles by the bayonet only; and yet at this weapon they would to a certainty be beaten by the Engliſh, were the forces on each ſide in every other reſpect perfectly equal; for their bayonets, which I have meaſured, are ſhorter, and worſe fitted for purpoſes of deſtruction, than ours. When they charge, nothing is more common than to hear them talk to each other, and fancy an Engliſhman, an Auſtrian, or a Spaniard, beneath their point, and crying for quarter.—I acknowledge freely, that the bravery of the French is as unqueſtionable as the light of the ſun; but this in itſelf is inadequate to the atchievements which we have recently witneſſed. To that lively courage which ſtimulates them to perpetual attacks; to their enthuſiaſtic ardour in the cauſe of their invaded country; and above all to their undiminiſhable numbers, muſt be attributed thoſe extraordinary events, which have confounded all political calculation, and filled Europe with amazement, conſternation, and mourning.

The preſent pay of the common ſoldier is

ten

ten fols a day and a ration of provifions, but no wine when quartered in towns. They are furnifhed by the ftate with neceffaries; fo that the money is for pocket expences only. The name of the general officer now commanding here is Klingly. He is a native of Alface, and one of the largeft men I ever faw, being at leaft fix feet four inches high, and proportionably ftout. I have once dined in his company, and fat next to him, when he told me, that he had been in England, and, among other parts of it, at Caftle Howard, the feat of Lord Carlifle; but in what capacity he had vifited there, he did not explain to me.—His birth is reported to be obfcure, and his advancement fudden.——— Adieu.

LETTER IX.

Quimper, 15th April, 1795.

BY a news-paper, which I lately read, I find
that the miseries and complaints of the
English prisoners here have at length been
communicated to our government; and that Sir
Morton Eden is absolutely arrived in France,
in order to negociate the terms of an exchange.
This subject, which I have forborne to touch
upon before, is a very serious one; and a relation of the sufferings which the prisoners of
war here have undergone, from the injustice
and cruelty of their treatment, would form a
most afflicting narrative. The following state-
ment, which was drawn up on the spot, by the
Honourable Mr. Wesley *, and transmitted to
Mr. Pitt, you may depend upon as a genuine
and faithful representation.

* Brother of the Earl of Mornington, who with-his
sister Lady Anne Fitzroy, was taken in a packet, by
French frigate, on their passage from Lisbon.

" In

" Quimper, 18th October, 1794.

" In the beginning of July laft, the prifons
" of Quimper contained about 2,800 fine young
" men, about which period a jail diftemper
" broke out among them, which has already
" carried off upwards of 1,200. This difeafe
" ftill continues to rage with violence, and is
" not to be attributed to any general ill ftate of
" the air, but to the following local circum-
" ftances.

" Firft—Want of cleanlinefs, from there being
" no neceffaries provided, whence the whole
" circumambient air becomes contaminated by
" fo many people.

" Secondly — Bad provifions, and thofe in
" very fmall quantities, the daily allowance for
" feven prifoners being only fix pounds of bad
" black bread; every fourth day thefe feven
" perfons receive alfo two pounds of falt pork
" among them; and on the intermediate days
" they are ferved with a fcanty mefs of horfe-
" beans. They have bad water, and no wine,
" or any fpirits of any kind; nor have even
" thofe who poffefs the means leave to pur-
" chafe thofe articles.

L 3   " Thirdly,

" Thirdly—Want of bedding and clothes,
" the commiſſary of the priſon of Pontenazan,
" near Breſt, having ſtripped the greater part
" of the victims, who had the misfortune to
" paſs through his hands, of their clothes, bed-
" ding, and money *.

" Fourthly—Want of proper hoſpitals and
" attendance on the ſick ; the hoſpital, which is
" intended for Engliſh priſoners, being too ſmall
" to receive half the number that are ſeized
" with the fever. The remainder are carried
" into a damp room, and laid upon ſtraw, with-
" out any covering; and the above-mentioned
" priſon allowance is their only ſupport.

" This is a fair and impartial ſtatement of
" the ſituation of our unfortunate countrymen.
" The winter, ſhould they remain here, will

* This commiſſary was ordered by the repreſentatives
then at Breſt, to take a blanket from each priſoner who poſ-
ſeſſed two, and to pay him for it. He executed this com-
miſſion by turning out of bed, into the court of the priſon,
all the priſoners, in the middle of the night, when he took
away *not half, but all their blankets*, without making any re-
compence whatever for them. Their complaints of this
robbery produced no notice or redreſs.

" open

" open a new scene of distress, as the few who
" may be spared, will then perish by cold and
" hunger, as they will be absolutely destitute of
" clothes, blankets, and other necessaries."

After this it were almost unnecessary to pursue
enquiry farther; but as some well-authenti-
cated anecdotes have been told to me, which,
besides their relation to the subject, strongly
tend to evince the temper of the times at
different periods, and thereby become in some
measure associated with the general politics of
the country, I shall give them to you, after first
premising, that I believe the greatest part of
these nefarious and disgraceful proceedings are
attributable not to a deficiency of either proper
liberality, or proper directions, on the part of
the present French government, but rather to
the villany. of their subordinate agents, who
have violated. the latter, in order to profit by
the former. We know that a *traitement*, in
assignats, to officers, who are prisoners, has been
decreed by the convention, and its rate settled;
although, from the multitude of offices through
which it has to pass, and the obstacles and impediments thrown in our way when we attempt

to trace the caufe of the ftoppage, hitherto we have not been able to recover any part of it. It is alfo fair to ftate, that fince a new com-miffary of prifoners has been appointed here, the daily ration of provifions, by being equitably iffued, is found very tolerably fufficient. Far-ther, in juftice to the people I am among, let me declare, that fince I have been landed (ex-cept a petty inftance or two of fplenetic infult) I have had no caufe to complain of oppreffive treatment, or to lament the want of as rea-fonable an extenfion of liberty as I could ex-pect.

I have faid, that in the winter bread was forbidden to be fold to the prifoners, and fo was fuel, notwithftanding the feverity of the feafon, and although no allowance of it was iffued to them. Had not the humanity of fome of the inhabitants of the town induced them to ftep forward to their relief, in defiance of the penalty of imprifonment, many of the Englifh muft have perifhed from cold.

The cafe of Lieutenant Robinfon, of the Thames frigate, will fet the conduct of the agents of tyranny in its proper light. This gen-

6   tleman

tleman was taken in the latter end of October
179.3, when *terror* was the *order of the day*, and
in the engagement, which led to the capture of
the ship, lost one of his legs above the knee,
and was severely wounded in the other. On
his arrival at Brest he was sent on shore to an
hospital, and attributes his being now alive to
a good constitution only; for he was neglected
by the surgeons, and obliged to eat food in the
highest degree improper for a wounded man.
He once applied to the chief commissary for
permission to send a person to buy some eggs,
vegetables, and other refreshments for him,
and was brutally refused. Mr. Robinson found,
however, in some nuns, who were compelled to
attend here, tender and careful nurses. These
poor women were subjected to the grossest in-
sults, and the harshest treatment. They had ac-
customed themselves, from motives of religious
commiseration towards the sick, to employ their
leisure hours in praying by the couches of those
who chose to hear them; but this pious and
humane practice was interdicted to them, by
an especial mandate from the representatives
on mission here; and two of them, who were
found

found guilty of tranfgreffing the order, were dragged to prifon, amidft reproaches, taunts, and execrations.

Some months after, when his cure was advanced, though far from completed, Mr. Robinfon, in a hope of changing for the better, requefted to be removed to Pontenazan prifon, about two miles from Breft, which was the general receptacle of the Englifh. Thither he was conveyed in a cart, with feveral more fick prifoners, and thruft into an old rope-houfe, containing 700 people, who fhortly after were increafed to 1,400. This room contained no beds for the fick, and his ftump was not healed. At firft they were allowed to walk for air in the day-time in an inclofed court; but this indulgence did not laft long, and thenceforth, on *no occafion whatever*, was a prifoner fuffered to go out of the room. Nay the windows were forbidden to be opened, though it was the beginning of fummer. However, upon this interdiction being communicated to the reprefentatives at Breft, they ordered the windows to be kept clofed on *one fide only*. This rigorous crowded confinement foon induced putrid difeafes,

eafes, which fwept off twenty and thirty perfons
a day, who were thrown without covering into
a large hole, and quick-lime heaped on the
bodies. The daily allowance of the prifon was
a pound and a quarter of black fandy bread,
four ounces of falt pork, a pint of four wine,
and at night a foup, of horfe-beans boiled in
water. The pork they were obliged to eat
always raw, for there was neither a kitchen, nor
any fire allowed, by which it could be dreffed;
and the fentinels were ftrictly forbidden to permit the prifoners to fend out and make pur-
chafes of fuel, or aught elfe that they might
need.

This huge dungeon contained people of all
ages. One day the commiffary of prifoners
pointed out to Prieur de la Marne (one of
the members of the convention on miffion)
fome little children, who were in a deftitute
miferable condition, and afked what fhould be
done to relieve their wretchednefs. " They are
" young vipers," cried this gentle and compaf-
fionate reprefentative, ftamping with fury, " turn
" them out to graze; grafs is good enough for
" the Englifh!"—This fame Prieur, who is now
" fhorn

" fhorn of his beams," and in arreft, is well
known for his feverities and oppreffions in Brittany. It feems, that he entertained hardly a
more favourable opinion of the people of Breft,
than of the Englifh; for at one of the meetings of the popular fociety there, after a great
execution, he affirmed that the town did not
contain three real patriots; and that all perfons who wore mourning for traitors (meaning
thofe who had juft been guillotined) were fharers
in their guilt.

On the 5th of laft May, Mr. Robinfon, with
other prifoners, was ordered to Quimper, at the
diftance of forty-five miles from Breft. A man
on crutches, who had but one leg, and that
crippled, might be fuppofed to be entitled to
the indulgence of a vehicle for his conveyance.
But when this unfortunate officer afked how he
was to be tranfported to the place of his deftination, he received for anfwer—" Walk, to be
" fure !"—In vain did he reprefent his utter
incapacity. He was commanded to fet out
with the other prifoners; and complied. At the
end of a mile he found himfelf totally exhaufted,
and muft have lain down to perifh on the road,

or

or await the cafual humanity of paffengers, had
not the foldiers who formed the efcort, lifted
him into a cart, which conveyed the baggage.
When they reached Quimper in a heavy rain,
they were all put, without diftinction, into an
old convent, and during the whole of this day
received for food and bedding—*ftraw* only.—
Finding himfelf wet and feverifh, and poffeffing
neither dry clothes or a bed, Mr. Robinfon requefted, as a favour, that he might be allowed
to fleep for the firft night at any houfe in town,
obferving to his keepers that he could not run
away; and offering, in cafe of compliance with
his entreaty, to defray not only his own expence, but that of the fentinel who might be
placed over him.—He was peremptorily re-
fufed.

Soon after Lady Anne Fitzroy, and her brother Mr. Wefley, arrived here. He who re-
collects the former courtefy and gallantry of this
once polifhed nation will fcarcely believe, that
an attempt could be made to immure a young,
helplefs, and beautiful woman, within the walls
of a common prifon. " The age of chivalry
" is indeed no more !" By much fupplication,
and

and after confiderable difficulty, her ladyfhip
obtained permiffion to hire an apartment in an
adjoining houfe, and to be ferved by a *traiteur*
with what fhe wanted for herfelf and her at-
tendants. She was, however, forbidden to hold
any communication with the people of the
town, and a fentinel was placed over her to enforce the order. In the procefs of her confinement, liberty of walking in a garden, at the
back of her prifon, was granted to her ladyfhip;
and this fignal indulgence was followed up with
leave to walk in the town, or to be carried in a
fedan which fhe had borrowed, guarded, however, by her fentinel, left her machinations
might endanger the republic. The humane
beneficence exerted by Lady Anne and her
brother, to all ranks of their poor countrymen
in captivity, are proclaimed here in terms of
the moft enthufiaftic applaufe and gratitude.
Mifery, in whatever fhape it appeared, excited
their compaffion, and called forth their bounty.
They fupplied the unhappy fufferers in the
common prifon with raiment, bedding, and
food, without which affiftance many of them
muft have perifhed.—You will obferve, by one
of

of my former letters (which, long ere this you moſt have received) that I had not the good fortune to fee her ladyſhip. Admiral Bligh was more lucky, when he carried his fon, in laſt January, on board the ſhip ſhe was in, to receive her protection. We have known, for fome time paſt, that they arrived fafely in England.

Were it neceſſary to continue the fubject, after what you have read, I am forry to fay, that it is in my power to adduce many more inſtances of premeditated fyſtematic neglect, cruelty, and oppreſſion, with which prifoners have been treated in this part of France during the prefent war. Many of the evils they have endured muſt indeed be placed to the account of Precini, the commiſſary, the fame blockhead whofe indecent democratic manners, in a company of ladies, fo much difguſted me foon after I came to this place. This man has at length been fuperfeded, and his office filled by a very plain honourable character, who extends to all in his department not only ſtrict juſtice, but every fair and confiſtent indulgence, which the ameliorated ſtate of public fentiments allows. The difmiſſion of his predeceſſor, which was of

the

the unceremonious kind, we chiefly owe to the reprefentations made by Captain Kittoe, who had long witnefled his iniquity, and combated it, after a long ftruggle, fuccefsfully. The defence which this gentleman made at the *club* (or popular fociety) of the town, before which he was denounced, for " harfh and unjuft ufage of " the prifoners of war," fhall, however, be recorded in his juftification. He did not deny that he had iflued to them bad and unwholefome provifions; but this, he faid, was only in compliance with orders he had received; in proof of which he named a reprefentative, who had publickly directed, that the ftore-houfes at Breft fhould be fearched for damaged bifcuit, " which," faid he, " is good enough for thofe " —— of Englifhmen!" Had the charges againft him turned on this fingle point, he muft, therefore, have been acquitted of them; but it was clearly proved againft him, that he had been guilty of innumerable acts of oppreflion and peculation.

While Precini locked up and cheated the prifoners, there were not wanting others to fport with their mifery. I dare fay you have

often

often read, in extracts taken from the Paris news-papers, of a noisy speaker in one of the sections, distinguished by his ridiculous assumption of the name of BRUTUS. This man is now a private sentinel, although but a few months since he was a general officer, and commanded the troops here. He was (like Tribout) originally a barber. During his command he took great delight in harassing the prisoners, and adding to their distresses. In one of these freaks an unlucky prognostic occurred of the decline of this great man's glory. Some Englishmen who had broken out of prison, in order to effect their escape, were retaken, and brought back. To amuse himself, Brutus ordered them to be shackled with the heaviest irons which could be procured, and in this condition marched them several times round the prison-yard; in the centre of which, encompassed by his satellites, he stood, enjoying their pain and aukward movements. A Guernsey-man, who was of the number, as they passed by the General, looked him full in the face, and cried, " *Chacun* " *à son tour.*" At the moment it caused only

M   an

an increafe of the univerfal merriment; but the
prediction feemed to be in fome meafure veri-
fied, when, foon after, Brutus's truncheon was
taken from him, and a mufquet put in its
place.

This letter will be forwarded to you by Mr.
Robinfon, the gentleman whofe name is fo often
mentioned in it. After a captivity of eighteen
months, he has received permiffion, in confideration of his wounds, to return to England, on
condition of fending back a French officer of
equal rank to himfelf.——Adieu.

LETTER

LETTER X.

Quimper, 30th April, 1795.

AT length the clouds of misfortune begin to separate, and a gleam of hope (though remote) breaks athwart the gloom, and points to England; whence I have lately received letters from thofe who are dearest to me, in which clafs I need not fay you are included. You were right to be fo brief and guarded in your expreffions ; although, as it happened, your letter reached me unopened, through a private channel. I obferve what you fay to me of the fteps you are taking to bring about my exchange. Several Englifhmen whom I know have lately effected theirs ; and to my great joy (though I fhall deeply feel the lofs of his fociety and protecting influence) the Admiral every day expects an order to arrive from the maritime agent at Breft, for his liberation. A Captain Courand, who, on the 1ft of June, commanded *Le Sans Pareil*, of 84 guns, is to be

M 2 exchanged

exchanged for him, and is now in France, pref-
sing the committee of public safety to ratify the
agreement, and forward the neceffary paffport.
You muft obferve, that Admiral Bligh is exchanged for a *Captain*, becaufe at the time of
our failing from England, in September laft, he
bore only that rank; in which capacity he commanded the Alexander, and confequently as fuch
only could be exchanged. Innumerable are
the obftacles which I forefee to prevent my
accompanying him, when his paffport fhall arrive; but, as I am on very good terms with the
commiffary, I fhall at leaft endeavour to obtain
leave to go to Breft, in order to folicit permiffion from the reprefentatives there to pafs over
into England, for the purpofe of procuring a
French officer of my rank to be returned in
exchange for me. If fuccefs attend my petition (of which I am not in utter defpair, as it
will be backed by the intereft of the Admiral)
I fhall be the bearer of my own letter; and if I
mifcarry, he will convey to you this fequel of
the adventures and obfervations of your friend.

Deprived as you are in England of all communication with this country, except through
the

the circuitous route of Switzerland and Germany, I often hear you afk me, What are the
prefent politics and fentiments of the French?
A man at the diftance of five hundred miles
from the metropolis can poorly anfwer fuch a
queftion; but if you will be contented with a
defcription of what the politics and fentiments
of the people of Quimper and its neighbourhood are, according to the beft information
which I can procure; and accept of a ftring
of opinions, derived from converfing with
ftrangers, and from reading news-papers and
frefh publications, as a folution of your enquiry, behold me ready to contribute to the
extent of my ability to your gratification.

Here the friends of royalty, federalifm, and
an undivided commonwealth, ftruggle againft
each other with reciprocal vibrations. Federalifm is, however, on the decline, and its fupporters,. attached as they are to the local prejudices which they contend for a continuation of,
perceive the impoffibility of carrying their point,
and are faft melting into the two other great
maffes. Royalifm, though bent to the earth, is
not crufhed. Its partizans are ftill numerous,

M 3 and

and its hopes fanguine, too fanguine, I fear, for
accomplifhment.   My political principles are,
you fee, unchanged fince we parted; and I ftill
think a limited monarchy the beft of govern-
ments.   Had I been born a Frenchman, I
fhould have ftruggled as hard for the revolution of 1789, as I fhould have refifted with all
my might that of 1792.   Much as I hate defpotifm, I am fcarcely lefs a foe to democracy ·
a fentiment which accords pretty well with thofe
of my royal friends here.   Since I have refided
among the French, I have met with only one
perfon, a lady (whofe hufband had once a place
in the houfehold, and has emigrated) who has
expreffed to me a wifh to fee the old fyftem reftored.   She, poor woman, cannot feparate the
fplendour of a court, and the unlimited power
of a king, from the profperity and happinefs of
the people, always defcribing the latter as a
direct and neceffary confequence of the former.
I am furprized to find that the royalifts prefer
Count d'Artois to his brother, Monfieur.   They
call the Count a bold and decided character,
although they do not fpare his former profligate
diffipation.   To the little Louis, " *le monarque*
" *au*

" *au berceau,*" as they call him, they look rather
with regret than expectancy, not unmingled with
apprehenfion, left violence or treachery fhould
be ufed againft him; but this fear I think
groundlefs, becaufe his prefervation will beft
ferve the intereft of thofe whom he is among.
I am affured that his morals are corrupted, and
his health deftroyed.—Unhappy infant! what a
leffon on the inftability of human grandeur does
he furnifh !

> " *Un faible rejetton——entre les ruines*
> " *De cet arbre fécond, coupé dans fes racines.*"
>
> HENRIADE, 7th Canto.

The royalift party is ftrongeft in the country,
and the republican in the town. The moft
numerous clafs of inhabitants in the latter, the
little houfekeepers, find their importance increafed, and their vanity flattered, by becoming
members of clubs and political focieties, and
being admitted into municipal pofts and honours. Doubtlefs, even in this part of France,
which has long been regarded with a jealous eye
by the government, the royalifts are not equal
in number to their formidable antagonifts :

they

they will, however, I am confident, fly to arms,
if ever a favourable opportunity of attacking
their oppreffors be prefented to them. Whenever I find myfelf (which fometimes happens)
in a little knot of thefe good people, almoft all
of whom have either fathers, brothers, fons, huf-
bands, or other near relations emigrated ; and
when I liften to the downfall of the convention,
and hear them, by the reftoration of a king, re-
ftore themfelves to their forfeited honours and
eftates ; it brings to my remembrance what
paffed, feventeen years ago, among the loyalifts
of Maryland, where I was then, as now, a prifoner of war. I hear fimilar fallacious calcu-
lations made, unfupported expectancies indulged, and ardent refolutions adopted, to end,
I fear, in fimilar difappointment. The paper-
money, divifions and miftrufts of parties, my
own fituation at both periods, and other circumftances, render the parallel very ftriking
to me. To dafh, with rude hand, the cup of
confolation from the lips of thefe unfortunate
people, were the extreme of cruelty ; but when
they appeal to me, by afking whether armies
of Englifhmen and emigrants may not be expeCted

pected to execute their airy fpeculations, I cannot become a partner of the deceit, by adminiftering to the delirium. Whatever might once be the opening prefented to us for the attacking of France in her vitals, by a co-operation with the armies of La Vendée, that feafon is paffed, never to return. To commence, at this declining period of the conteft, fuch a fyftem, were almoft to proclaim, that while we believed it poffible to fubjugate France by a coalition of exterior force, we difdained to profit by the arms of Frenchmen, in a caufe which we called their own. Befides, if a publication, which is ftuck up in all parts of the town, dated the 1ft of *Floreal*, at Rennes, and figned by ten reprefentatives, and twenty-two *Chouan* chiefs, with Caumartin at their head, may be believed, the Vendeans have made their peace, and fubmitted to the republic, after having for more than two years caufed the moft powerful diverfion in favour of her external enemies. But this my friends here intreat me to defpife; and, when I point out to them its marks of authenticity, affure me, that Charette will never lay down his arms, but on

the

the condition of royalty being re-inftated; that
he is only temporizing, and will foon break out
ftronger than ever.   I liften in filence, and
know not which way to turn my faith.—What
fhall I fay of this extraordinary character, Charette ! who, whatever be his future intentions,
has hitherto, certainly, difplayed extraordinary
powers of mind, and Antæus-like arifen frefh
from every fall.   I am acquainted with two
people who perfonally know him, and defcribe
his talents, courage, and perfeverance, in terms
of enthufiaftic admiration.   The French do
not fcruple to affirm (but here I fufpect their
love of exaggeration, not unmixed with national
vanity, to preponderate) that the war of La
Vendée has coft to the republic more men
than all her foreign conflicts united.   If, inftead
of men, perplexity and vexation were fubftituted, the account would be more credible.

The proclamation which announces a conclufion of the war of La Vendée is not the only
one, which ftrikes at this moment the public
eye, in Quimper.   His Pruffian Majefty, Fre-
deric William, our good and faithful ally, has,
we are told, alfo made his peace with the republic.

public. When I recollect his threatening bom-
baftic language, and the mighty irruption made
into Champagne, not quite three years ago, by
this pigmy in the fhoes of a giant, I can compare him to nothing but the month (April) I
write in, which is faid to come in like a lion and
go out like a lamb. The French themfelves
cannot help adverting to his former menaces,
and fneering at them, when compared with his
prefent meeknefs and tender concern for the
effufion of human blood. The preamble of
the proclamation ftates, that, " in Pilnitz, a
" part of his Pruffian Majefty's dominions, the
" firft partitioning treaty of the territory of
" France was executed. That now the repub-
" lic has demonftrated to kings and minifters,
" that fhe is not only victorious but invincible,
" fhe will prove to them that fhe is generous,
" and willing to grant peace, upon terms con-
" fifting with her dignity, to all her enemies.
" And, that henceforth the ftability of her go-
" vernment, not only to conclude, but to gua-
" rantee, treaties and alliances, ought not to be
" doubted, &c. &c."— A peace with Spain,
x   likewife,

likewise, is reported to be in great forwardness; so that it is probable, before the end of this year, England alone will have the contest to maintain; and well, I trust, it will be maintained by our victorious fleet?

If then the coalition be on the point of its dissolution, and Charette has laid down his arms, either we must abandon the subjugation of France, or seek for other means to accomplish it, which, if they exist at all, are internal. Nothing can be more dazzling and imposing than the great success of the French against their foreign enemies, and the seeming ease with which the vast machine of the republican government moves; but this smooth exterior conceals a hollow and ulcerated inside. The numberless abuses subsisting in the multiplied public offices, which defy control or abolition; (what think you of its being asserted in the convention, that in the post - office department more than *thirty-nine thousand* persons receive salaries?) the depreciation of *assignats*, which proceeds in a ratio continually increasing, a piece of money, which eight weeks since sold for 140 livres, now fetching 400, and, above

all,

all, the enormous public expenditure, which almoft defies computation; are caufes of the moft ferious alarm to the fupporters of the revolution. The laft of them, if not checked, muft produce a national bankruptcy, and overturn this government, as it did the monarchy; but whether to give birth to a new form of democracy, or to the reftoration of a king, who fhall fay!

By the report of the new financier, Johannot, made to the convention—

	livres.	
The national expence of the month of *Nivofe* laft was - - -	423,374,450 - or -	£. 18,522,632
The receipt of taxes in the fame month was - - - - -	57,168,733 - or -	2,501,132
Excefs of expenditure, rejecting fhillings and pence, and reckoning a livre at 10½d. - - - -	366,205,717 - or	£. 16,021,500

In the fucceeding month, *Pluviofe*, the difference was ftill more enormous: it exceeded the receipt by 443,164,244 livres, or £. 19,388,435. "The trappings of royalty" would poorly keep pace with this unprecedented profufion, which is hourly increafing, by the inevitable augmentation of falaries to all the

the public servants, both civil and military. The naval officers have had a considerable addition to their pay since I left Brest, and, as a signal to all beneath, the stipend of the members of the convention has been increased from eighteen to thirty-six livres a day.

I do not pretend to know the nature and extent of the present taxes; but I remember the favourite scheme of a heavy land-tax, in lieu of all others, was trumpeted forth at the commencement of the revolution, not that it dates its birth at so recent a period. Our principle of taxing consumption, they treated with great contempt; but I have reason to believe they will soon adopt it, as I have lately read a most spirited and ingenious attack on Cambon, and some of his predecessors, in which it is extolled. The most considerable of the present imposts is a duty of 20 *per cent.* on all lands and houses. This was calculated to produce 260 millions, and makes the annual value of landed property (including buildings) to be 1300 millions of livres. Let us suppose (dreadful supposition!) that a third part of this is sequestrated, and in the disposal of the government.

ment. Call this 440 millions; and farther, let
us prefume, that all thefe houfes and lands will
be fold at 25 years purchafe (which, if the
nature of a part of the property, and the fears
of reclamation, particularly of the eftates of the
later emigrants, be confidered, is perhaps too
much) the amount will be 11 milliards. This
is the calculation of the moft fanguine of
the French with whom I have converfed on
the fubject; and even this, terrifying as it is to
compute or read, feems likely to be infuffi-
cient. Johannot reckons the national means
at 15 milliards 226 millions, even· after the
allowances, which juftice and humanity dictate,
fhall be deducted from them; and propofes to
coin immediately 150 millions of copper, in
order to afford fupport to the declining credit of
affignats. I need not tell you, that I poffefs no
data to formally controvert this ftatement of
the financier; but I beg leave to obferve, that
his whole report, which I have carefully read, is
conceived in thofe fanguine and flattering terms,
which appear to me to have fprung from a
pre-concerted determination of exhibiting the
favourable fide of the picture, and keeping the
                                        people

people in good-humour. I have heard it publickly derided, and have been told that both
its premifes and conclufions are falfe. In addition to the allowance which he hints is to be
made to the relations and creditors of emigrants,
under certain reftrictions, is to be placed a
complete reftitution of the properties of the
Briffotine party, and all who fuffered under the
tyranny of Robefpierre: at leaft fuch expec-
tations have been holden out in the convention.
He alfo ftates, that there are now eight milliards
of *affignats* in circulation, and that only three
milliards more need be added to them. For
the juftnefs of this laft declaration his word
muft be taken, as he does not tell us why he
limits to this fum the future emiffion.—Query,
How are the creditors of the old government
to be confidered, when the day of liquidation
fhall arrive ? A lottery, it feems, is projected,
of all the forfeited houfes; and the fcheme, at
leaft here, appears to be relifhed. — There is
yet another fource of revenue, of a delicate nature, which I fometimes hear and read boafted
of: — requifitions from the conquered countries;
and confifcations of the church lands in the
                                        Auftrian

Auftrian Netherlands.—How far thefe will be practicable to any great amount, I leave to you to determine. Remember, that the comparatively trifling levies, which have been already made upon the Belgians, are faid to have rendered the French name odious in that country.

But little facts fometimes imprefs conviction on the mind, when a laboured detail has failed. —Until lately there were not any *affignats* in circulation of more than two thoufand livres each in value; but, on the petition of the army contractors, *affignats* of ten thoufand livres each have been fabricated, " in order to leffen " the *expence of carriage*, which is become " enormous."—One of the Paris papers, two months ago, affigned as a reafon for raifing its price, the increafing value of paper, which was then 80 livres a ream. " How," afks the editor, " can it be otherwife, when govern- " ment, by contract, is every day fupplied with " fix thoufand reams for its confumption in " printing off *affignats* !! "

All *affignats* of the value of more than 100 livres, bearing the effigy of Louis XVI. were profcribed fome time fince, except in the pur-

N   chafing

chafing of national domains. This was one
of the laft piratical manœuvres of Cambon,
and was every way worthy of the financier of
Robefpierre. However it fomewhat contri-
buted to leffen the immenfe load of circulating
paper.

When I fum up the component parts of this
ftupendous fyftem, and contemplate it in the ag-
gregate, I muft confefs myfelf to be ftaggered,
and almoft ready to pronounce againft the ability
of this wonderful people to continue the conteft
in which they are engaged. But, after revolving
the fubject in every point of view in which it
prefents itfelf to my mind, I am decidedly of
opinion, that not even a national infolvency
would produce the effect, which fome of the
powers combined againft them fought in its
commencement. The difmemberment of France
cannot be accomplifhed, without the extermi-
nation of its inhabitants, even though Mr. Play-
fair write a fecond profound difquifition to demonftrate its neceffity and practicability; and
how far a " *bellum internecinum*," againft twenty-
four millions of people is either in its principle
to be defired, or in its accomplifhment to be
expected,

expected, may at leaſt exercife the cafuiſtry of humble fearchers of truth, like you and me.

That the French wifh for peace, cannot be doubted by thofe who are in a habit of reading their daily chronicles, and liſtening to their fentiments; but even this event, defirable as they feel it to be, they will not purchafe at the expence of the integrity of the empire, or by fuffering any power, or combination of powers, on earth, to dictate to them what ſhall be their form of government, or even to interfere in the moſt inconfiderable point about their internal regulations. Such, upon my honour, I believe to be the unalterable determination of a large majority of the French nation. A peace with us they efpecially covet. I ſhall not now ſtay to examine what are the impediments on our fide to its completion. We are accufed of wiſhing to monopolize the trade of Europe to both the Indies. According to the lateſt accounts I have read from one of them, notwithſtanding our rapid conqueſts in the beginning, the tide of victory feems to be fo far balanced, as to render the event dubious; and even if we finally fucceed in that quarter, it may be-

N 2   come

come a queftion, whether " *le jeu vaut la chan-*
" *delle.*" The yellow fever, and the refiftance
of a million of men, fuddenly awakened to a
perception of their rights, are antagonifts not
to be defpifed. " Emancipate the negroes, and
the commercial afcendancy of England is for
ever deftroyed," faid Danton. My opinion is
very different; and I am perfuaded, that if the
Charibean iflands were at this moment inde-
pendant ftates, our fhipping would not be lefs
numerous (for our immenfe capital would flow
into other channels) nor would fugar, rum,
coffee, and Barbadoes water, be lefs attainable
to adminifter to our luxury. If the opulence of
England be founde on the bafis of African
flavery; if the productions of the tropies can
be difpenfed to us only by the blood and tears
of the negro, I do not hefitate to exclaim—
" Perifh our commeree;" let our humanity
live !

By the way, I am often afked, why we joined
againft them in a confederacy, whofe aims (they
fay) were as irreconcileable to each other, as
to juftice. This query I have fo little fatisfaction in anfwering, that for the fake of argu-
ment,

8

ment, and to prevent being totally overborne, I retort it upon them, and accufe them of being the aggreffors : a conteft in which nothing is gained or loft, for both affirm, and both deny.

It is, neverthelefs, certain in the mean time, that a hatred of us, as a nation, is univerfally diffufed among the favourers of the revolution. When declaiming on this head, their extravagance is fometimes not unentertaining. They have collected, and believed, without examination of their abfurdity, a number of wild and ridiculous tales about us : fuch as that there exifted a fcheme to fet the Duke of York upon the throne of France ; that Marat and Robefpierre were in the pay of Mr. Pitt, and acted by his directions, &c. &c. They ftun one, indeed, with repetitions of the name of Mr. Pitt, and execrations of his politics, which, I often tell them, is the higheft compliment they can pay him. " His father," faid an orator in the convention, " infufed into him, in his " infancy, his hatred of France, and, like Hamil- " car of old, fwore him to eternal enmity againft " the French name." But, perhaps, another

N 3   great

great man, whofe fhare in provoking the war, and founding the knell of peace, has not been inconfiderable, may feel difappointed on being told, that his name in this part of France is never mentioned, and is even unknown. The fplendid pebble, with which Mr. Burke, after the firft revolution, endeavoured to perturb the lake of French tranquillity, has not yet fpread its undulations to this diftant fhore.—To de-fcend from Mr. Burke to his vaunted antagonift Tom Paine, I was, on coming into France, cu-rious to learn what had become of this wander-ing demagogue, whom the delirium of the mo-ment had rendered confpicuous. For a long time I could get no intelligence of him: to fome his name was new; and others, with dif-ficulty recollecting it, faid he was guillotined. My enquiries remained unfatisfied, until I chanced to read in a news-paper a decree of the convention for his releafe from arreft, with other deputies of the party of Briffot. From this time, until a few days fince, I had ceafed to think about a being, whofe name was never mentioned; when a news-paper again prefented it to me, in a report of Courtois to the con-vention,

vention, dignified by the title of "founder of
"liberty in the two worlds." Notwithſtanding
this conſolatory panegyric, I am of opinion
that Mr. Paine is not deſtined to ſhine on the
theatre of French politics. But whither ſhall
he retire to better his fortune, and re-lume his
fame? America would *now* prove a ſterile and
unproductive ſoil for the tranſplantation of
ſuch a genius; while ungrateful Europe (the
French dominions excepted) ſhutting every
avenue againſt him, bids him wander, like a
ſecond Cain; without an aſylum, or a reſting-
place.

To return to my ſubject.—The preſent period
is certainly an intereſting one in the hiſtory of
the revolution. The convention is not popular,
and every day loſes ground in the affection of
the people. You can form no adequate idea
of the cloſeneſs with which its proceedings are
ſcrutinized, and the aſperity with which they
are attacked, in the news-papers, and in private
circles. Since I have reſided among the French,
freedom of opinion and ſpeech has made an extraordinary progreſs. Heads which, ſix months
ago would have " 'bided but the whetting of

N 4   " the

" the axe," now declaim unintimidated, and unreftrained. Has the propofition of Merlin de Thionville, for the diffolution of the convention, and the election of a national affembly, yet reached you? It was ftrongly defended, and ftrongly reprobated. For the prefent, Merlin has been prevailed upon to withdraw his motion; but, I think, it will be refumed foon: the royalifts eagerly long for it, and predict, from the moment it fhall be decreed, the reftoration of monarchy, provided the election be free and general; but this is not expected, as a propofal, in cafe it muft be adopted, has been already ftarted, to oblige the people to elect a majority of the prefent legiflators. In the mean time the new conftitution is loudly clamoured for by the republicans. Sieyes, who is at length emerged from behind the curtain which had fo long concealed him, and others, are faid to be preparing it; and a very beautiful metaphyfical theory of impracticability, I doubt not, it will prove. Let this be as it may, I dread an agitation of thefe queftions, and become doubly defirous to get out of France before they are ftarted; for, during the time

of

of the election, we shall at least be locked up and half starved, if no worse befal us.

But another question, which involves more important consequences than at first appear, *viz.* Whether the leaders of the ancient committee of public safety, Barrere, Collot d'Herbois, and Billaud de Varennes (Vadier having escaped) shall be tried, or not? has during the last six weeks almost absorbed every other consideration. It was, in fact, an experiment of the strength of the two parties, the moderates and terrorists, which divide the convention. The latter are generally supposed to be completely overthrown; but, in my opinion, the middle step, of inflicting, without a trial, the punishment of exile (some say to Cayenne, others to an island on the coast of Brittany) upon culprits whose crimes exceed credibility, is not only unjust, but evinces something like a compromise. The royalists, the Brissotines, and all others who have been lately freed from confinement, greatly dreaded the escape of these monsters, in the consequent triumph of their party. Poor Madame Kérvélligan, while it was pending, did us the honour, with some

more

more ladies, to dine with us. You cannot
picture to yourself terror like her's, left the
moderates should be defeated. She took from
her pocket a paper, and read to us from it, with
great encomiums, the speeches in the convention of Legendre, Isnard, and others who had
declaimed against the *prevenus*; while she was
enraged in an equal degree against those who
had defended them, and resisted the return of
the proscribed deputies (her husband is of the
number) into the bosom of the convention, until
they should be purified by trial. Lecointre of
Versailles was not spared upon this occasion.
Mr. Kérvélligan is now in Paris; and who can
wonder at her perturbation? Of the seventeen
months which he lay concealed, she was shut up
eleven a close prisoner in the château of Brest.
If she do not hear from him by every post, she is
miserable; not knowing, in the present temper
of the times, who may be spared in a popular
commotion. She and others declared to me,
while the struggle lasted, that so exasperated
were the two parties against each other, that
they should not be surprized to hear, that they·
had had recourse to arms, and butchered one
another

another in the fenate-houfe. The days and nights
of the 12th and 13th of *Germinal* were particularly terrible. The convention during the
whole of them remained at its poft, moft of
the members being armed with piftols to prevent affaffination. In this commotion, of which
part of a narrative, written by one who was
on the fpot, has been read to me, the cry of
" *Vive Louis dix-fept!*" was once or twice heard,
but it was faintly uttered, whilft " *Vive la re-
"publique*, and give us a conftitution!" refounded on every fide.

Immediately after this difturbance was quelled, expreffes communicative of the event were
difpatched into all the diftricts. The courier
to this place arrived a little before noon on
the 9th inftant, and the drum was forthwith
beat in every quarter of the town, inviting all
" *good citizens* " to repair at two o'clock to the
cathedral, to hear the account from Paris read,
and to adopt meafures in confequence of it.
Being affured of not giving offence, I went at
three to the place of appointment, and found
the municipality, and about 150 people of the
lower order, including a few officers, feveral
                                        foldiers,

foldiers, and many women, collected. They
were liftening to a man who was mounted into
the pulpit, and reading to them a *bulletin*, ftating
the circumftances of the attempt which had
been committed on the national reprefentatives,
and of its fuppreffion; alfo the names of certain
members whofe arreft had been decreed; and
laftly, that General Pichegru was called in, to
preferve by an armed force the peace of Paris
from the machinations of royalifts and terrorifts. Every body wore their hats, and no infult
was offered to us Englifhmen, feveral of whom
were prefent. When the reading was finifhed,
an addrefs to the convention was voted, on the
patriotifm and energy they had difplayed; and
feveral people got into the pulpit, and fpoke in
their turns. From thefe orators, a blackfmith
was univerfally allowed to bear away the palm,
haranguing with great fluency againft the terrorifts, and furprizing his auditors by the keennefs
of his farcafms, and the juftnefs of his obfervations. The fpeech of one who afcended the
tribune was fimply, " *Vive la republique !*" which
was received with many plaudits. In conclufion they decreed, that the members of the ancient

cient committee of *furveillance* of the town
(which has long been fuppreffed) fhall be
deemed fufpected perfons, be difarmed, and
obliged to appear every day before the municipality; and that henceforth they fhall not be
eligible to any office of truft or power in their
commune.

A mention of the committee of *furveillance*
leads me to bring you acquainted with that in-
fernal inftitution, which, of all engines that ever
were placed in the hands of a government, was
furely the moft effectual to over-awe the citizens,
and to promote the caufe of defpotifm. The
number and coft of this hoft of licenfed fpies
were not lefs extraordinary than their power,
which authorized them, without affigning any
reafon but a fufpicion of incivifm, to enter the
houfes of all the inhabitants, whom they pleafed
to fay had been denounced to them; to feize
upon their perfons, in order to deliver them
over to the revolutionary tribunal; and to break
open their cabinets, and infpect their papers.
There are in France forty thoufand communes, and every commune had its committee,
which, upon an average, contained ten members,

bers, the number in part depending upon that of the inhabitants. The falary of every member was five livres a day.

If therefore we multiply - -	40,000
by	10
the number of members will be	400,000
	5
and the expence per day - -	2,000,000 livres ;
which multiplied by - - -	365
makes the annual expence - -	730,000,000 livres, or, at

10½ d. each, £.31,937,500.

The committee of *furveillance* of Quimper confifted of twelve members, whofe names and occupations were as follows :

Botibon, retail fhopkeeper,	Rofe, - barber,
Harier, butcher,	Roland, - merchant's clerk,
Moreau, mufician,	Morivan, - hog-butcher,
Becam, taylor,	Le Moine, gardener,
Cariou, taylor,	Montaigne, brazier,
Keroch, barber,	L'Hot, - printer's devil.

They were to a man the creatures of the creatures, ten gradations deep, of the committee of public fafety. In fuch hands were
the

the liberties and lives of Frenchmon depofited! Even on the day I write, the inftitution is not totally abolifhed, but is momently expected to be fo. It is ftill retained in towns which contain forty thoufand inhabitants, or more, but is feldom allowed to exercife its powers.

The number of perfons guillotined in Quimper was only four, two priefts and two women. The *guillotine* was kept in the cathedral, but performed its office on the parade. It was cuftomary to fend to Breft thofe who were denounced, which was more convenient than to try them on the fpot, where witneffes might have eftablifhed their innocence: of this clafs there were many victims. I was told, when at Breft, that 172 perfons of both fexes had been executed there. The operation is faid to have been performed on 32 of the number in fomewhat lefs than nineteen minutes.

It is impoffible to pronounce the word *guillotine*, without affociating with it its grand mover Robefpierre, that modern Procruftes, who fought to contract or extend to the ftandard of his own opinion, a mighty people; before whom neither elevation of virtue or talents could erect a

shield,

fhield, or infignificancy of birth and fituation
creep beneath a fhelter. Without aiming to
become his defender, I muft, however, be permitted to obferve, that many of the relations,
which, on authority feemingly good, I every
day hear and read of his towering ambition and
capricious cruelty, are too extravagant to be
credited, and, if true, too degrading to our nature to be repeated.   In the general horror and
indignation excited by his remembrance, I am
fenfible (efpecially among this declamatory
people) that truth will often be facrificed to
paffion.   There is, befides, a fecond reafon,
that increafes the diftruft with which I liften :—
to fcreen themfelves from odium, all the fubor-
dinate tyrants fix upon him, and attribute to
his orders, the innumerable butcheries and acts
of oppreffion which they have perpetrated.—
They who were once his clofeft imitators, are
now loudeft in their outcries againft his memory ; which, in many inftances, is loaded with
the crimes of his contemporaries.   I had not
been taken twenty-four hours when Captain
Le Franq, either from credulity, or a wifh to
imprefs me with an early belief of his not being
                                          attached

attached to a finking party, told me, among similar tales, that Robefpierre had, in the town-hall of Paris, caufed himfelf to be proclaimed, " Maxmilian the Firft, Emperor of the " French." Upon finding that a man, whofe relative rank and fituation in life entitled him to refpectable fources of information, could thus, either from ignorance, prejudice, or a lefs laudable motive, be guilty of fo grofs a mifreprefentation, it became doubly incumbent upon me to reftrain my belief.

However outrageous the execrations of the French now are on hearing his name, they do not furpafs the adulation with which they once approached the idol of his power. I wifh I could fend to you the *Gazette Nationale* of the 30th of *Pluviofe*, which belongs to a collection of news-papers that I have accefs to, and contains a report of the 16th of *Nivofe*, made to the convention by Courtois, in the name of the committee appointed to examine the papers of Robefpierre. Never before was flattery fo grofs and fervile ufed as fome of thefe productions, which were addreffes to him from different diftricts, *communes*, and popular focieties. The

O ftatue

ftatue infcribed to the "*immortal man*," and
the poetic incenfe afterwards offered at his
fhrine by Boileau, fade before it.   He is called
in them the glorious, incorruptible Robefpierre,
who covers, as with a fhield, the republic by
his virtues and talents; who joins to the felf-de-
nial of a Spartan, or a Roman of early date, the
eloquence of an Athenian.   Even his tendernefs and humanity of difpofition are praifed.
One man congratulates himfelf on a perfonal
refemblance of him; and another, at the diftance of 600 miles, is haftening to Paris, to
feaft his eyes with a fight of him.   He is compared, not by an individual but by a body of
people, to the Meffiah, "*annoncé par l'Etre Su-*
"*preme, pour reformer toute chofe*;" and afterwards he is faid to manifeft himfelf "*comme*
"*Dieu, par des merveilles.*"   On fome occafion
a *Te Deum* was performed for him, the burthen
of the ditty being, "*Vive Robefpierre! Vive la*
"*Republique!*"—I feel afhamed to tranfcribe any
more of thefe impious and contemptible abfurdities.   I beg of you, however, to remark, when
Courtois's report fhall fall into your hands, that
amidft the papers which have been fcrutinized

of

of this extraordinary perfonage, though incon-
trovertible evidence of his reftlefs and fanguinary difpofition appears, yet nothing bearing
the marks of an arranged plan for mounting a
throne, or erecting himfelf into a dictator, was
found. Some trifling hints are once or twice
thrown out, which the reporter does not fail to
magnify; but Robefpierre, if he ever really
entertained fuch a project, was too circumfpect
to commit it to writing; and knew too well
the loofe nature of man to entruft his fecret,
until it were matured in his own mind, and
could tempt to confederacy by its probability
of accomplifhment. I never reflect on the
fudden and total apoftacy of the French from
this man and Marat, without indulging a
hope that the verfatile levity of fentiment,
and unceafing defire of change, which cha-
racterize the nation, will at length point, in a
fpirit of repentant loyalty, founded on an un-
conquerable determination to be free, to the
defcendants of their kings. And this hope
I am always willing to fuftain, by calling to
mind our reftoration of Charles the Second;
but at the fame time I confefs, that (at leaft

for

for the prefent) my obfervations pronounce it
to be rather a conclufion which I defire, than a
confummation which I expect.

By pofterity then muft Robefpierre be judged. No fcrutiny will reach his virtues, however it may exalt his genius. Vigour of mind
he undoubtedly poffeffed, and he joined to it
(except in moments of inebriation, to which he
was fometimes addicted) profound diffimula-
tion; but there exift unqueftionable proofs,
that he was a poltroon, which fingle flaw in his
compofition rendered his downfall certain. A
combination of other caufes might have prolonged his elevation, but could not have pre-
ferved it to the end of his exiftence. On how
many occafions did Cromwell's perfonal intrepidity, and firmnefs of nerve, uphold him and
his authority!

We owe candour more to a review of the
worft than of the beft of characters; and no
man was ever more entitled to an indulgence
of it than Robefpierre.

The papers of the other members of the
committee, of which Robefpierre is believed to
have directed all the fprings, are alfo laid open,
§   and

and are equally curious and fhocking as his. There are among them orders, ready figned and fealed, for bringing to trial, and executing, thofe whofe names might be inferted in the blank fpaces. Juries, a venerable inftitution derived from *us*, have hitherto had very little claim to the gratitude of the French. In a report made to the convention by Saladin, in the name of the committee of 21, on the 13th of laft *Ventofe* (3d March) it is ftated, that the managers of the committee of public fafety, Barrere, Collot, Billaud, &c. held every evening conferences with the public accufer and the prefident of the revolutionary tribunal, who rendered to them an account of their proceedings, and received their inftructions for the work of the next day.—On the following account you may alfo rely. A judge and jury were fent to Paris, from a place 200 miles diftant from it, to give an account of their principles, for having condemned two men to ten years imprifonment, who, in the opinion of a reprefentative who was prefent in the court, ought to have fuffered death. The crime of the prifoners was, having faid, that " they

O 3   " wifhed

" wifhed to fee the tree of liberty of their com-
" mune cut down."—The fentence was ordered
to be quafhed; they were tried again; and
guillotined.

An extract of a letter, figned Darthè, found,
after his execution, in the cabinet of Le Bas,
is as follows. " *Le comité de falut public a dit à*
" *Le Bon, qu'il efperait que nous irions tous les*
" *jours de mieux en mieux. Robefpierre voudrait*
" *que chacun de nous pût former un feul tribunal,*
" *et empoigner chacun une ville de la frontiere.*"
After this gentle wifh (allowing it to have been
uttered) which breathes more clofely that of
Caligula than any other that modern biography
affords, you will, perhaps, think I have been
too lenient to the memory of Robefpierre.
Remember, I only wifh to apportion his fhare
of guilt. The convention, by banifhing the
triumvirate, " until they can be tried at a
" period of more tranquillity," not only demonftrate a fear of the Jacobin party, but a fecret
apprehenfion left many of themfelves fhould
be implicated in the tranfactions which fuch an
enquiry would unfold. Hence the violent op-
pofition to a publication of their papers by

*   many

many of the moderate party, as well as that of their opponents. How indeed, in confiftency, could thofe men, from whom they derived their powers, now turn their accufers?

To conclude an odious and debafing fubject. The " *noyades, fuzilades*, and *republican mar-* " *riages*" of Carrier at Nantes; joined to the exploits of Collot d'Herbois at Lyons, who chained together, at one time, four hundred people, in the great fquare of the city, and fired upon them with grape-fhot, until they were ex-terminated; with many others equally diabo-lical, which fhall not pollute my page, almoft tempt one to believe, that a majority of the nation were at one time accomplices in its crimes and miferies. They have, indeed, at length awakened from their delirium, and figh at the dreadful retrofpect.

I have written until my paper is exhaufted, my eyes bedimmed, and my imagination haunt-ed by racks, wheels, and *guillotines* dyed in hu-man gore.—Therefore good night! and adieu until to-morrow, when I will refume my pen!

LETTER XI.

A MIDST fuch fcenes as I was yefterday condemned to defcribe, it were impof- fible but an univerfal corruption of manners muft follow, and it has accordingly arrived. That the French fhould pant to be free, who can doubt, or who can blame? But it has happened to *them*, as it muft to every people who are fuddenly hurried into extremes, with- out the national mind being in any degree pre- pared for the change which has taken place. This people poffeffes not the ftability of cha- racter, or the auftere felf-denying virtues, of the ancient republicans. Many of the prefent leading demagogues of the convention do not even affect a common regularity of manners ; and, if the public journals, which do not fpare them by name, may be believed, wallow in the moft fcandalous fenfuality. I read the other day a defcription of a drunken fcene between

one

one of the Merlins and a brother deputy, which
was pourtrayed with much humour. I mention
this to fhew you, that the editors of news-papers
here are not more afraid of the executive power
than on your fide of the water. When I compare the prefent number of the convention to
what it was at its inftitution, not three years
fince, and recollect the caufes,—felf-murder,
public execution, defertion, and banifhment—
which have occafioned the diminution, I ftand
petrified with amazement and horror. What
ftronger proof of the depravity of this legifla-
tive affembly can be adduced than their perpetual deliberate acts of treachery towards each
other, in betraying private converfations, which
have paffed among themfelves? Their annals
are full of it. How many of their members
have been hurried by it to the *guillotine*; and
how many more have been fupplanted in the
public favour by the informers!

The thirft for diffipation is not leffened; but
whence the means which enable many of the
French to purfue it in its prefent form are derived, is a myftery. If the exceffive and daily
increafing price of commodities be confidered
nothing

nothing is more inexplicable than how thofe
who have only ftipulated incomes contrive to
fubfift upon them. I live with the moft rigid
frugality, and yet cannot bound my expences
within lefs than 250 livres a week. It is certain that falfe *affignats* abound ; and the tongue
of malevolence has not fcrupled to affert, that
many of them have been iffued from the national treafury, " in order to leffen the public
" debt, when the day of prefentation for pay-
" ment fhall arrive." Remember, I do not
pretend to ftate this as more than the whifper of
party. It is evident that the habits, which this
plenty of the medium of exchange, however
obtained, creates, are deftructive of all induftry.
This little town is crowded by men and women,
who, like the Athenians, do nothing from morning to night " but tell and hear of fome new
" thing." The national ficklenefs demonftrates
itfelf no lefs in private than in public opinion.
In Paris alone, in the month of laft *Nivofe*, 223
divorces took place, 198 of which were folicited by the *wives*. Nothing is more fpecious
than a facility of divorce. To render the chain
of union indiffoluble were, indeed, to realize
the

the punifhment of Mezentius; but to permit its
feparation upon every trifling and momentary
caprice, is to corrupt fociety in its fource.
You know that marriage is here a civil
contract only, which I have feen entered into
at the *bureau* of the municipality, and which
confifts merely in the parties declaring, before
certain witneffes, their wifh to be united, and
entering their names in a regifter; but of late
all but flaming republicans have thought it neceffary to ftrengthen the engagement, by privately fuperadding the ceremony of the church.

The national tafte has fuffered equal degradation. The dramas of Racine, and the odes
and epiftles of Boileau, are fupplanted by crude
declamatory productions, to which the revolutionary fpirit has given birth. The French
have been almoft as ingenious as ourfelves.
It was a difcovery referved for the prefent age,
that Pope was a mere verfifier; and that the
immortal compofitions of the two before-men-
tioned writers are harmonious tinklings only,
devoid of fire of fancy, and elevation of genius.
There has been a report prefented to the convention, on the *Gothicifm* which has overfpread
the

the land, and exterminated in its fury more than two thirds of the works of art and tafte, which ennobled France. It will be handed down to pofterity, in the chronicles of the revolution, as a fact that marks the fpirit in which it has been conducted.

Notwithftanding the various arms by which religion has been perfecuted, fhe again begins to lift her head. A report, prefented by Boiffy d'Anglas, from the united committees of public fafety, general fecurity, and legiflation, to the convention, containing ten articles in favour of public worfhip, has been adopted and decreed. By thefe the republic acknowledges no national religious inftitution; nor grants falaries to the priefthood; nor furnifhes any place for the performance of worfhip, &c. &c.; but it exprefsly forbids, under pain of punifhment, every one from preventing his neighbour from the exercife of his devotion.

In confequence of this decree on the back of the proclamation iffued by Guefno and Guermeur, and of affurances from the conftituted authorities that they fhall not be molefted, the moderate catholics here affemble on every Sab-

bath

bath in the cathedral, the ufe of which (as an indulgence) is granted to them; but the more rigid, fearlefs of the law (which forbids it) hold little meetings at each other's houfes, where the non-juring clergy officiate. This is known to the police; but the predilection of the country people, who flock in great numbers to thefe affemblies, renders it convenient to wink at them, and has hitherto reftrained all attack upon them.

I went upon Eafter Sunday to the cathedral, and found a numerous congregation there. The altar was lighted up by twelve large waxen tapers; the holy water was fprinkled upon the congregants; and the incenfe was burnt, with the accuftomed ceremonies; but even here democratic fpleen manifefted itfelf in difturbing what it is no longer allowed to interdict. In the moft folemn part of the fervice, the *Marfeillois Hymn* was heard from the organ: that war-whoop, to whofe found the bands of regicides who attacked their fovereign in his palace marched; and which, during the laft three years, has been the watch-word of violence, rapine, and murder!

murder *! How incongruous were its notes in the temple of the Prince of Peace! A black-guard-looking fellow clofe to me, whom I knew, by his uncombed hair, dirty linen, ragged attire, and contemptuous geftures, to be a *veritable fans-culotte*, joined his voice to the mufic, and echoed, " *Aux armes, citoyens!*" Fear alone kept the people quiet; and of its influence in this country I have witneffed aftonifhing proofs, which demonftrate, beyond volumes of reafoning, the terror infpired by the revolutionary government.

As the obfervance of the Sabbath advances, the *Decadis* fink into contempt. I had heard much of civic feafts and other patriotic inftitutions celebrated upon them; but fince I have been here, nothing of the fort has occurred. The national flag is difplayed on the public offices, and if there is no preffure of bufinefs,

* I was once carelefsly humming, at a fire-fide, the *Carmagnole*; when a lady, fuddenly interrupting me, exclaimed, " For God's fake ceafe that hateful tune! It " brings to my remembrance nothing but maffacres and " guillotines."

the

the clerks have a holiday. A few zealous republicans alfo fhut up their fhops; but at prefent for one fhop fhut on a Decadi, there are fix on a Sunday; for, however their owners may differ on political queftions, a fenfe of religion is not extinguifhed in the mafs of the people, even of the town. I have, neverthelefs, been affured, that fix months ago, to have fhewn this mark of refpect for the Sabbath would have been a certain mean of drawing down the refentment of the predominant faction. On every Decadi the laws are appointed to be read in the cathedral, and the municipality attend. I had once the curiofity to go to this meeting, and found the number of auditors, which I counted, exclufive of the reader, and thofe who attended officially, to be twenty-feven perfons, of whom, to my furprize, five were old women.

Were I not bound to attend an appointment at twelve o'clock, in the event of which I am deeply interefted, methinks it were a curious fpeculation (to which I incline) to try to develope what will be the probable ftate of France, when peace with all her neighbours fhall be reftored to her. The thinking part of

the

the nation furvey, not without alarming anticipation, the confequence of a million and a half
of armed men, to whom a habit of indolence is
become familiar, being turned loofe upon a
country whofe fpecie has difappeared, whofe
foreign commerce is annihilated, and whofe
manufactures muft be *born again*, for hardly a
trace of their having ever exifted remains : add
to this, that the government, by being no longer
revolutionary, will lofe its ftrong executive
fpring : and that the people are fplit into innumerable parties, which hate each other with
irreconcileable inveteracy.

National prejudices and political antipathies
I confider as a vile ftate engine, which, in the
hands of a few crafty men, has for more than
five thoufand years wrought the milery of the
human race. Englifhmen and Frenchmen, the
Charib and the Hindoo, the philofopher of
Europe and the naked favage whofe wander-
ings I have witneffed at Botany Bay, fhall one
day, I prefume in humble confidence to truft,
be affembled before the " living throne," of a
common Father ; and look back on that diminutive fpeck, which in the boundlefs ocean of
infinity

infinity nothing fhort of divine irradiation could make vifible to their eyes;—to review with un-qualified contempt, forrow, and repentance, thofe falfe principles, and fanguinary conclu-fions, which rendered it unto them a theatre of contention and horror, and caufed their days to be " few and evil!"

If fuch be my fentiments, I have no right to wifh calamity to France. I do not.—May fhe conclude peace with her neighbours; and la-bour to fettle her own government; and render happy her numerous children! But when I look forward to the completion of fuch an event, I think I forefee fo many long years of havoc, which have yet to urge their courfe in this devoted country, that I will drop the curtain, and haften to meet —— ——. Adieu.

P   LETTER

LETTER XII.

MY DEAR ———,   Plymouth, 11th May, 1795.

CONGRATULATE me. The circumftances
which led to my obtaining permiffion to
come to England, prove me fortunate beyond
example; and as I think them honourable to
French generofity, I fhall not omit to record
them.

I arrived here yefterday, in a little Danifh
brig bound to Copenhagen, which ran off the
Sound, and made a fignal for a pilot.   One of
the Cawfand boats in confequence pufhed out
to us, and received Admiral Bligh, his two
young gentlemen, and myfelf.   We were foon
landed; and I am happy to tell you that I found

——— ——— ——— ——— ——— ——— ——— ———

——— ——— ——— ——— ——— ——— ——— ———

The packet which accompanies this will explain to you my hopes, and the meafures
which I intended to purfue, at the time it was
written.   The Admiral's liberation and paffport
arrived

arrived on the 2d inftant; and, on his requeft
for his *aid-de-camp* and interpreter to accompany him, the good commiffary made no fcruple
of furnifhing me with a paffport to go to Breft,
upon pledging myfelf to return, in cafe my application to the reprefentatives might be re-
jected.   Having bidden adieu to my friends, I
fet out on the following morning on horfe-
back, with the Admiral and the two boys in a
carriage, the beft the town afforded, without
fprings, and with traces made of ropes.   Our
fudden departure was in confequence of knowing that an embargo, which had fubfifted for
fome time, was juft taken off, and that feveral
American veffels were ready to fail for England   We travelled about thirty-fix miles,
through a country which is full of young pro-
mifing corn, indicating a plentiful crop, and
appearing not to have fuffered from wanting
hufbandmen to fow it.   About four o'clock
we reached a village, whence there is a ferry
about ten miles acrofs to Breft.   Here we embarked, with more than a dozen country people,
who were carrying the produce of their farms to
the next day's market.   Only one of them could

P 2   fpeak

speak French, who satisfied the curiosity of the
rest about us. They made their supper of
crape, and were abundantly thankful to us for a
remnant of a piece of cold veal which we had
brought with us, some bread, and a little wine,
which they ate as luxuries. Owing to a con-
trary wind, it was midnight before we got
abreast of the harbour's mouth; when we learned, by hailing a vessel, to our unspeakable mortification, that all the Americans had sailed in
the course of the day. The circumstance of
having missed, by being a few hours too late,
an opportunity, the fellow of which might not
arrive for months, joined to the apprehensions
and perplexity of men in our situation, on entering into a garrison-town like Brest, at so un-
seasonable and suspicious an hour, rendered our
feelings very unenviable. We wanted the boat-
men to land us at the town, and to shew us to
an inn, where we might be accommodated with
beds; but this they peremptorily refused to do,
telling us, that we might every moment expect
to be hailed by one of the forts, and ordered
on shore to give an account of ourselves. This
happened, as they had foretold, in a few minutes,

nutes, when we were fummoned through a fpeak-
ing-trumpet to land within fome pallifades at
the point of the dock-yard. A ferjeant and a
file of men received us, and conducted us immediately to their officer at the guard-houfe, a
tall well-looking young man; who after having
infpected our paffports, and liftened to our
wifhes, very civilly offered to accommodate us
as well as he could in his guard-room, or, if this
propofition were not agreeable, to fend a ferjeant with us to knock up an inn. We were
grateful for his politenefs, and begged to accept
the latter, requefting permiffion to leave our
baggage under his care until morning, which
was complied with, and a ferjeant was directly
fent away with us. We had, however, but juft
paffed one of the barriers of the dock-yard,
when we were ftopped by a municipality pa-
trole, who, notwithftanding our conductor's ex-
planations and remonftrances, carried us all
forthwith to their guard-houfe, and gave us to
underftand, that we muft pafs the night there
as well as we could. This treatment enraged
us; and I bade them recollect that they were
offering an unneceffary indignity to a " *General*

P 3 " *Anglais*,"

" *Anglais*," who had not entered Breſt without ample and ſufficient authority, and who would certainly repreſent their interference and impertinence, on the next morning, to his friend Admiral Villaret, and the members of the convention on miſſion here. This reſolute tone, to which the Admiral deſired me to give full force, had quickly its effect, and this *bourgeois* collection of tinkers and taylors thought proper to ſend us under an eſcort to a neighbouring inn; but it was now become ſo late, that, after having knocked at the door for more than half an hour, we were obliged to return to the guard-houſe, and take up our lodging there: the Admiral ſitting up, on a bench, by the fire, and the two youngſters and I lying down on the guard-bed with the ſoldiers.

In the morning we took our leave with very little ceremony, and repaired again to the inn, where we found admiſſion. After breakfaſting, and rendering our dreſs as decent as we could without our baggage, we went, as we had been directed at Quimper, to the office of the maritime agent, and produced our paſſports. He received us very properly, and furniſhed us with

tickets

tickets to fhew in cafe of being ftopped—an
event not unlikely to happen to Englifh officers walking in their uniforms about the
ftreets of Breft. Our next vifit was to Monfieur Villaret, whofe reception of Admiral Bligh,
and whofe undeviating conduct to us both while
we remained here, was friendly, polite, and flattering in the extreme. I had never before feen
him, and had now the honour to be introduced
to him by Admiral Bligh, as his *aid-de-camp*.
His frank and gentlemanlike manners at once
won my efteem. He appears to be between forty
and fifty years old, is of an engaging counte-
nance, well made, of a middle fize, and has a
military carriage. Upon hearing where we had
left our baggage on the preceding evening, he
directly difpatched his own coxfwain for it, and
it was brought to us fafe and entire. But his
goodnefs to me (as the friend of an officer
whom he fo highly refpected for his gallant defence of his fhip, as Admiral Bligh) muft be
particularly ftated to you. No fooner was the
predicament in which I ftood made known to
him, than he offered his intereft to back my application to the reprefentatives; and infifted that

P 4 we

we all fhould immediately fet out to their
office to undertake it. Upon our arrival there,
we were introduced to one of them, Champeaux, an old man, who at Admiral Villaret's
interceffion confented at once, without ftarting a
difficulty, to my being allowed to accompany
my Admiral, and promifed me a paffport.

Our only difficulty now was to find a conveyance. Admiral Bligh therefore expreffed a
wifh to his friend that he might be fuffered to
hire a boat, which he would engage to fend
back immediately on being landed on the neareft
part of the Englifh fhore. This propofition
(which, confidering the times, was rather of a
delicate nature) was acceded to by Monfieur
Villaret; who added, that he would take care
that fhe fhould be properly fitted and victualled
for us: however in the afternoon a lucky oc-
currence prevented us from putting his generous zeal to ferve us to farther proof:—An
American gentleman, who knew our fituation,
brought a little Danifh mafter of a brig to our
inn where we had dined (Admiral Villaret being
engaged to the reprefentatives) with whom we
prefently concluded an agreement for our paffage.

fage. As the Dane wifhed to depart on the next
day, it became again neceffary to trouble Monfieur Villaret to urge the completion of our
paffports for failing out of the harbour; and for
this purpofe he appointed to meet us at nine in
the evening, at the houfe of the reprefentatives.
Thither, at the hour agreed upon, we repaired,
and found him. He conducted us into a fpacious garden, and introduced us to the reprefentatives, Topfent, Vernon, and Harmand, who
received us with great cordiality; and when they
learned that Admiral Bligh had been all day in
town, chided Admiral Villaret for not having
brought us with him to dine with them. Thefe
gentlemen, however, declined taking any part
in granting the paffports until the arrival of
their colleague Champeaux, who was momently
expected. We, therefore, continued walking
on the terrace, and converfing on general fub-
jects, which unavoidably led to the grand and
only enquiry that feems to agitate the minds
of Frenchmen:—the politics of the day, as
connected with the revolution.—They fpoke in
refpectful terms of our national character, and
pathetically lamented the war between England
                                              and

and France, calling it an unhappy and fruitlefs conteft to both parties. It was, they faid, paft human comprehenfion to account for the ceafe-lefs implacable enmity between two nations, which by their valour, opulence, and enlight-ened character, were fitted to hold the balance, and dictate the tranquillity of Europe. I liftened in filence. Thefe men had no *fans-culottifm* about them, either in their manners, language, or drefs; the two firft were civil, moderate and correct, and the latter was gentlemanlike and refpectable. Had it been my defire, it was not my intereft, to interrupt or oppofe them. I ventured, however, once or twice to flightly demur at one of their propofitions, in order to draw out their fentiments more fully; which oc-cafioned thefe words (from Vernon, I think) to be repeated with emphafis, " *France will be a* " *republic! and England neither fhall, nor ought* " *to, interfere in our internal concerns.*" This converfation made a deep impreffion upon me, and was, I am confident, introduced in order that the Admiral (to whom I interpreted it) might communicate it on this fide of the water. It differed but little from others which I had

often

often heard on the fame fubject during my captivity; but the rank and fituation of the fpeakers
from whofe lips it fell, render it memorable to
me.—Finding that Champeaux did not come
home, about ten o'clock we retired to our inn,
being firft given to underftand, that I might be
fure of meeting him in his office at fix o'clock
next morning, being the hour at which he always entered upon bufinefs.

At a few minutes before fix on the following
day I renewed my vifit, and waited but a fhort
time before I was admitted to Monfieur Champeaux. He was fitting in his office, in an el-
bow-chair, dreffed in a flannel jacket abomi-
nably filthy, and fmoking a fhort black pipe,
exactly fuch an one as the old women in Ireland carry about in their mouths. It brought
to my mind Sir William Temple's defcriptions
of thofe old burgomafters, who formerly, with
fo much plainnefs, wifdom, and integrity, conducted the affairs of the Batavian republic. I
had no more reafon to complain of my reception now than on the preceding day. He told
me that he did not wonder at my impatience,
and that I fhould wait for what I wanted only
                                                    until

until a clerk fhould come in. " But," added
he, " our clerks are *fainéants*." Ah! thought
I, if this honeft gentleman could take a peep,
at this early hour, into an Englifh public office,
where vigilance for the common weal never
flumbers!—His affable compliance removed a
mountain from my mind. I now took an opportunity of prefenting Admiral Bligh's compliments to him, and requefting, as an acknow-
ledgment of his politenefs, that he would name
fome French officer, a prifoner in England,
whofe releafe he might be interefted about,
and that he might depend on his being fent
home. The old man bowed, and, recollecting
himfelf for a moment, wrote down the name of
a *Quarter Mafter*, who was taken in l'Atalante
frigate, and is now in prifon at Kinfale in Ireland, begging that I would give it to the Admiral with his thanks, and perfect reliance on
his good faith. I continued to wait; but no
clerk entering, although fome other company
did, I flipped out, and planted myfelf on the
ftair-cafe, where I had not remained long before a grave fober official-looking character
came forward.—" Pray, fir," faid I, " do you
                                        " belong

" belong to the office?"—" Yes, citizen."—I
told him my bufinefs in few words, and having
been fimilarly fituated in an Englifh office,
when I begged his affiftance, looked as if I
would be *grateful.*   " Are you fure, citizen, that
" you have feen the reprefentative?"—" Per-
" fectly fure."—" The reprefentative Cham-
" peaux?"—" Yes."—" Then follow me, and
" your bufinefs fhall be done."—With a bound-
ing heart I accompanied him into his office.
When he had finifhed writing the paffports, he
took them in to the reprefentative to be figned
and fealed, and I amufed myfelf as well as impatience, not unmingled with fear, left fome un-
forefeen impediment fhould be ftarted, would
allow, by looking about the room in which I
was left alone.   Oppofite the door was written,
in large characters, " Whatever fervant of the
" republic fhall accept of a fee or gratuity, for
" tranfacting the public bufinefs, fhall forfeit his
" place, and be farther punifhed."   There was
alfo ftuck up on the wall a fatirical print of certain characters among us, who fhall be name-
lefs, in very ludicrous attitudes and fituations.—
He foon returned with the paffports completely
executed,

executed, and prefented them to me, in fuch à manner as convinced me, that to have offered a reward to him, for having fimply performed his duty, would have been conftrued into an infult, and perhaps have been attended with unpleafant confequences to myfelf.

I hurried to the Admiral with my credentials, and we loft no time in getting on board, and urging our departure from the port, which to our unutterable joy took place about eleven o'clock laft Tuefday. A northerly wind pre-vented us from arriving here till yefterday.

The fhortnefs of my refidence in Breft, and the ftate of hurry and anxiety in which it was paffed, almoft preclude me from offering to you any remarks about it. It is very ftrangely laid out, on the fide of a hill, and long flights of fteps connect different parts of the town. It is cer-tainly much larger than either Portfmouth or Plymouth, and contains fome handfome public buildings, exclufive of the naval arfenal, which, you may be fure, I did not enter after the firft night, when it was too dark to make any obfer-vations. The French are faid to be making vigorous preparations here; but when we ran

through

through Breft-Water, there were only nine or ten fail of the line ready, or nearly ready, for fea. As we failed along, I caft a look of exultation at my old jail La Normandie. At the harbour's mouth we were boarded by a guard boat, the officer of which offered not any interruption to us, upon feeing our paff-ports.

I had almoft forgotten to mention that before we embarked we heard that Le Franq, the captain of Le Marat, was cafhiered, for being a *Robefpierrift*; and that he, with many others was obliged to fhew himfelf twice a day at the office of the municipality, as a caution againft his elopement. We did not fee him, and by no means thought him entitled to much com-miferation.—Admiral Villaret gave us the infor-mation.

To the civility of Mr. Anderfon, the Ameri-can conful, we were indebted, not only now, but when we were formerly at Breft. My two old friends of the prifon-fhip, on hearing of my arrival, found me out, and came to fup with us at our inn.

Our expences ran very high during our fhort

ftay

ftay at Breft. We dined, at a very middling ordinary, at fifteen livres a head; and for tolerable
wine after dinner were charged nineteen livres a
bottle; every other article being proportionably
extravagant.

I wait here only for ——— ——— ———
——— ——— ——— Expect to fee me in
town in a week.———Adieu.

WATKIN TENCH.

T H E   E N D.

For EU product safety concerns, contact us at Calle de José Abascal, 56–1°, 28003 Madrid, Spain or eugpsr@cambridge.org.

www.ingramcontent.com/pod-product-compliance
Ingram Content Group UK Ltd.
Pitfield, Milton Keynes, MK11 3LW, UK
UKHW010336140625
459647UK00010B/646